2011 RENWICK CRAFT INVITATIONAL
history in the making

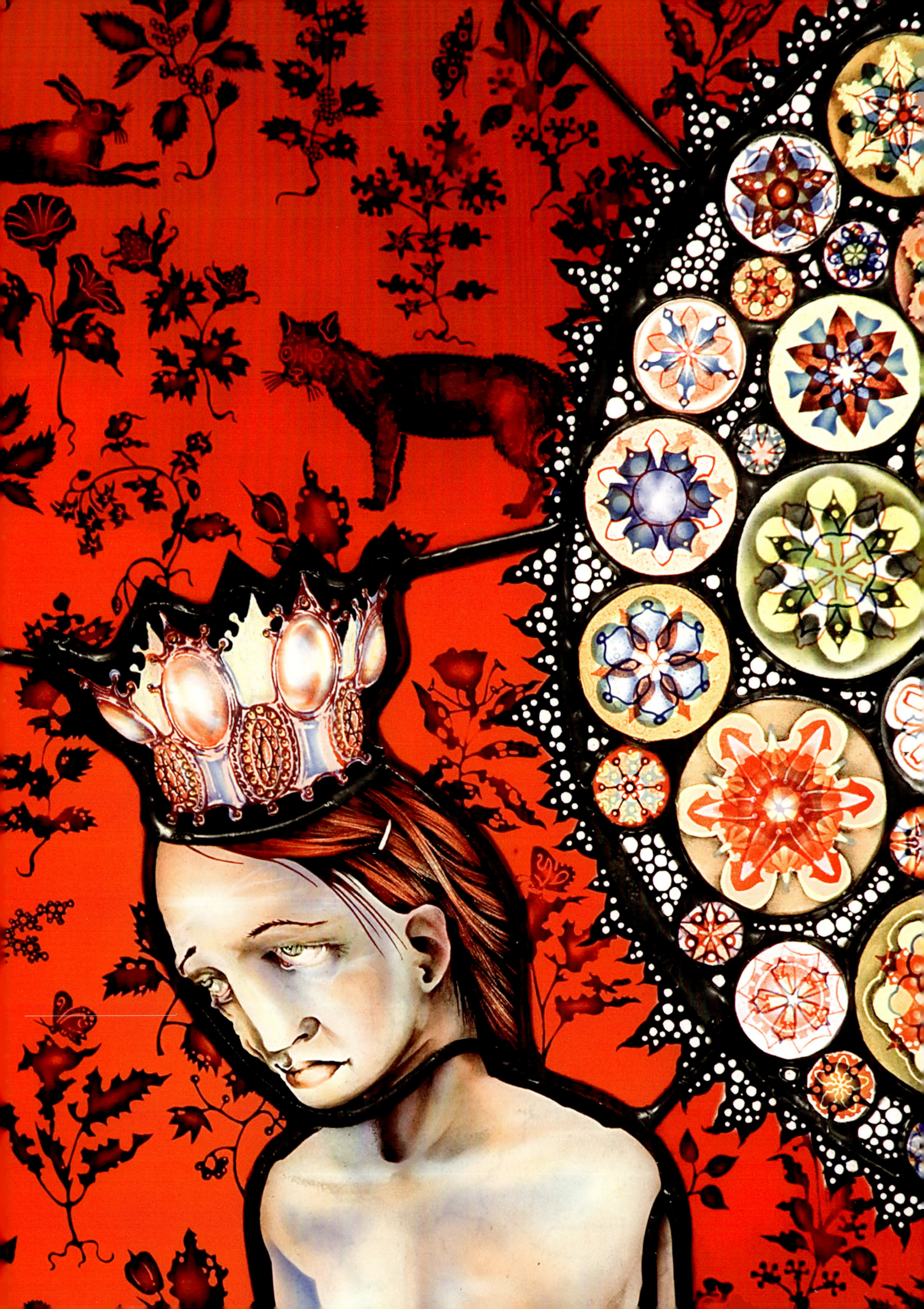

2011 RENWICK CRAFT INVITATIONAL
history in the making

written by
nicholas r. bell
ulysses grant dietz
andrew wagner

foreword by
elizabeth broun

Renwick Gallery of the
Smithsonian American Art Museum
Washington, DC

in association with
Scala Publishers Ltd

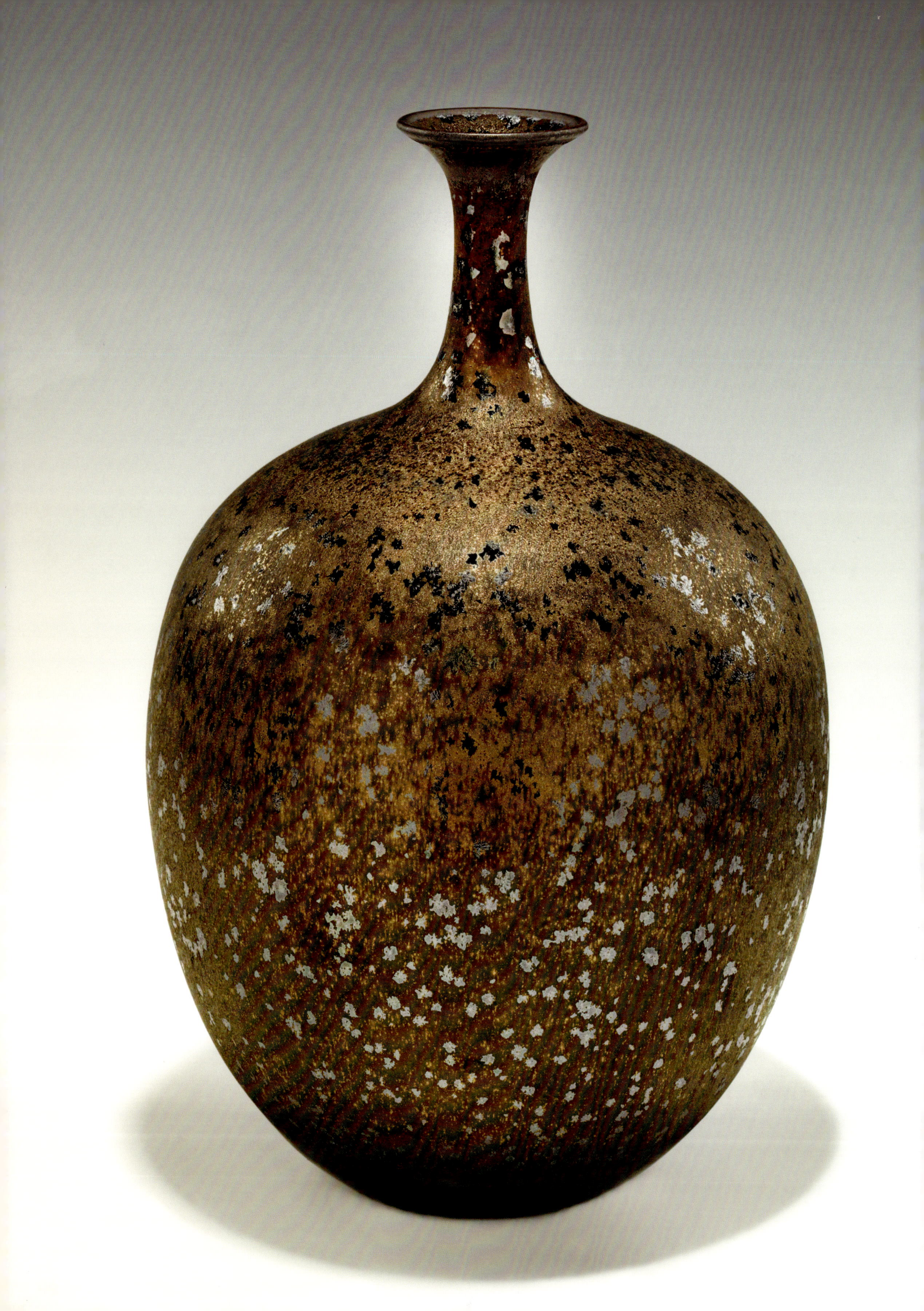

The Ryna and Melvin Cohen Family Foundation Endowment provides generous support for *History in the Making: Renwick Craft Invitational 2011*. The Cohen Family's generosity in creating this endowment makes possible this biennial series highlighting outstanding craft artists who are deserving of wider national recognition.

History in the Making: Renwick Craft Invitational 2011
By Nicholas R. Bell, Ulysses Grant Dietz, and Andrew Wagner, with foreword by Elizabeth Broun

Chief of Publications: Theresa J. Slowik
Editor: Mary J. Cleary
Designers: Karen Siatras, Jessica Hawkins
Photographer: Gene Young

Published by the Smithsonian American Art Museum in association with

Scala Publishers Ltd
Northburgh House
10 Northburgh Street
London EC1V 0AT

Printed and bound in Singapore

The Renwick Gallery of the Smithsonian American Art Museum collects, exhibits, studies, and preserves American crafts and decorative arts from the nineteenth to the twenty-first century. Housed in a historic architectural landmark on Pennsylvania Avenue at 17th Street, NW, the Renwick features one-of-a-kind pieces created from clay, fiber, glass, metal, and wood.

The Smithsonian American Art Museum is home to one of the largest collections of American art in the world. Its holdings—more than 41,000 works—tell the story of America through the visual arts and represent the most inclusive collection of American art of any museum today. It is the nation's first federal art collection, predating the 1846 founding of the Smithsonian Institution. The Museum celebrates the exceptional creativity of the nation's artists whose insights into history, society, and the individual reveal the essence of the American experience.

For more information or a catalogue of publications, write to:

Office of Publications
Smithsonian American Art Museum
MRC 970, PO Box 37012
Washington, DC 20013-7012

Visit the Museum's Web site:
AmericanArt.si.edu

Smithsonian American Art Museum
Renwick Gallery

Library of Congress
Cataloging-in-Publication Data

Renwick Craft Invitational (Exhibition)
(5th : 2011 : Washington, D.C.)
History in the Making : Renwick Craft Invitational 2011 / Written by Nicholas R. Bell, Ulysses Grant Dietz and Andrew Wagner ; Foreword by Elizabeth Broun.
pages cm
"Published in conjunction with the exhibition of the same name, on view at the Renwick Gallery of the Smithsonian American Art Museum, Washington, DC, March 25-July 31, 2011."
Includes bibliographical references.

ISBN 978-1-85759-703-5 (softcover)

1. Decorative arts—United States—History—21st century—Exhibitions.
I. Bell, Nicholas R., author.
II. Dietz, Ulysses G. (Ulysses Grant), 1955–author.
III. Wagner, Andrew (Andrew Allen), 1973–author.
IV. Renwick Gallery. V. Title.
NK808.2.R45 2011
745.0973'074753—dc22

2010049691

Cover: Ubaldo Vitali, *Tureen* (detail), 2001, silver and sodalite. Collection of the artist (see p. 31, top)

Frontispiece: Judith Schaechter, *My One Desire* (detail), 2007, glass. Collection of Todd Alios VonBastiaans (see p. 71)

Page 4: Cliff Lee, *Luster Oilspot*, 2010, porcelain and luster oilspot glaze. Collection of Carol A. Weiser and George H. Weidner, Jr.

Back cover: Cliff Lee, *Table Set*, 2002–8, porcelain and celadon glaze. Collection of the artist

contents

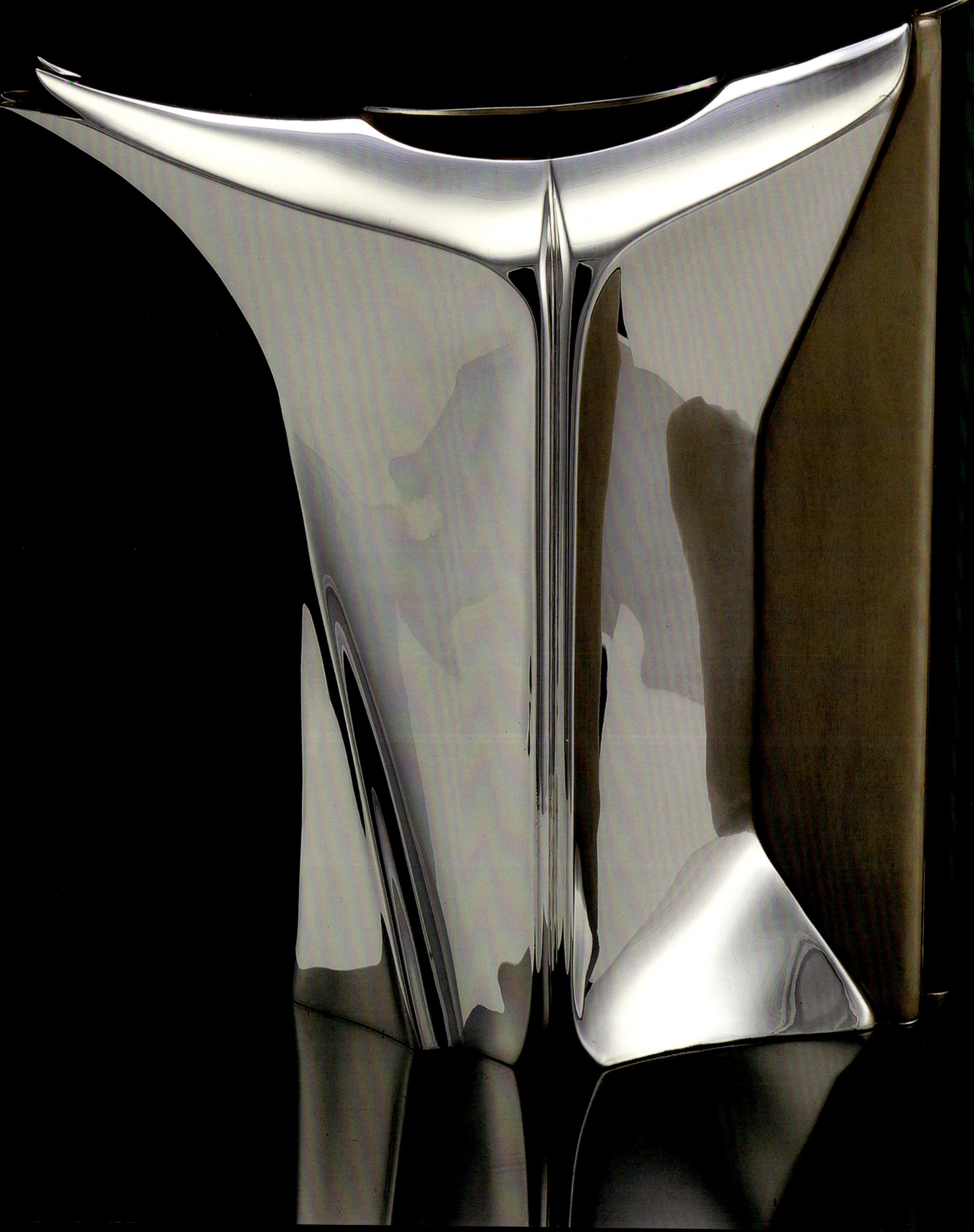

foreword

The Renwick Craft Invitational is now an established tradition, known around the Museum by its nickname, the RCI. Thanks to the Ryna and Melvin Cohen Family Foundation, this biennial exhibition is a stable feature of our museum landscape, a wonderful presentation held every other year to celebrate craft artists deserving of wider national recognition. After a decade, we have earned the right to put roman numerals after the title, so I am calling this show RCI V!

I love the subtitle of this fifth exhibition in our series, *History in the Making*. It captures the thrilling way crafts recall some "remembrance of things past." For me, a contemporary vessel is more resonant when it "remembers" the distinctive profile of an Athenian krater or a pilgrim's flask. And Cliff Lee's exquisite porcelains are more meaningful when I know he spent seventeen years searching for the secret of imperial yellow glaze. Judith Schaechter's stained glass windows remind me of the hours I spent as a student of medieval art, transfixed by the brilliant rose windows in France's cathedrals. Ubaldo Vitali's dazzling silver services walk me back through the dynasties of kings and their bravura displays of fanciful tabletop silver settings. Matthias Pliessnig's woven bentwood furniture first reminds me of wicker pieces made for a future planet, then makes me think of Viking ships sailing to discover the New World. These four artists have the history of their media embedded deeply in their subconscious, so their work feels at once profoundly rooted and entirely fresh.

Another title for this show could be *Past Perfect*, linking the love of tradition to the intense and exquisite perfection of the workmanship of these artists. A colleague commented recently that "there's a lot of

Ubaldo Vitali, *Pitcher*, 1988, silver, bleached maple, and glass. Collection of the artist

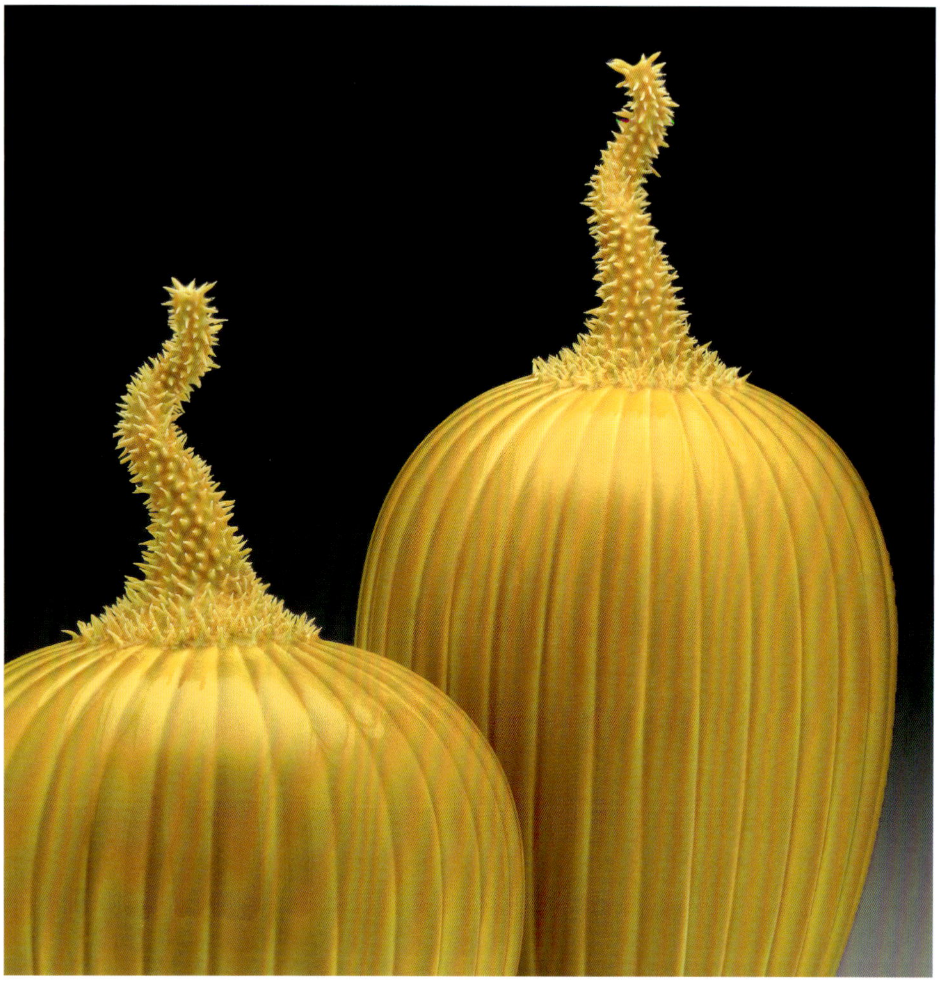

Cliff Lee, *Prickly Melons* (details), 2008 (see p. 47)

obsession in the craft field," which is an understatement. One work in the exhibition by Matthias Pliessnig, *Rivulet,* has more than seven thousand points of contact, each joint locked with a tiny bamboo peg. Does Pliessnig have more than twenty-four hours in his day, to permit such laborious perfection in his work? Contemporary craft artists have wowed us for decades with the wizardry of their techniques, so we expect breathtaking skill as a norm. But the artists in this exhibition set a new standard even within that tradition. These Fearless Four challenge every limit, experiment with new ways of working, and invest countless years in refining their art. The "margin of difference" narrows as they come ever nearer perfection, but still they demand more of themselves, even at the summit. It excites me to know that these artists are working way beyond any of our "expectations" and are focusing instead on their own challenges, however open-ended a commitment this requires. This aspect of their art includes a spiritual component and a philosophy about what matters in life, which I admire.

Each of the five RCI exhibitions has had a selection panel to choose the artists and a curator to shape the project. Each exhibition and book reflects the perspectives and tastes of its creators. The previous Invitational featured artists determined to break the boundaries of craft by staging theatrical scenarios in their art. This one is different, a more classic response to the high drama of 2009, committed to deep traditions and exciting materials, transformed by extraordinary ideas and unparalleled skill.

ELIZABETH BROUN
The Margaret and Terry Stent Director
Smithsonian American Art Museum
October 2010

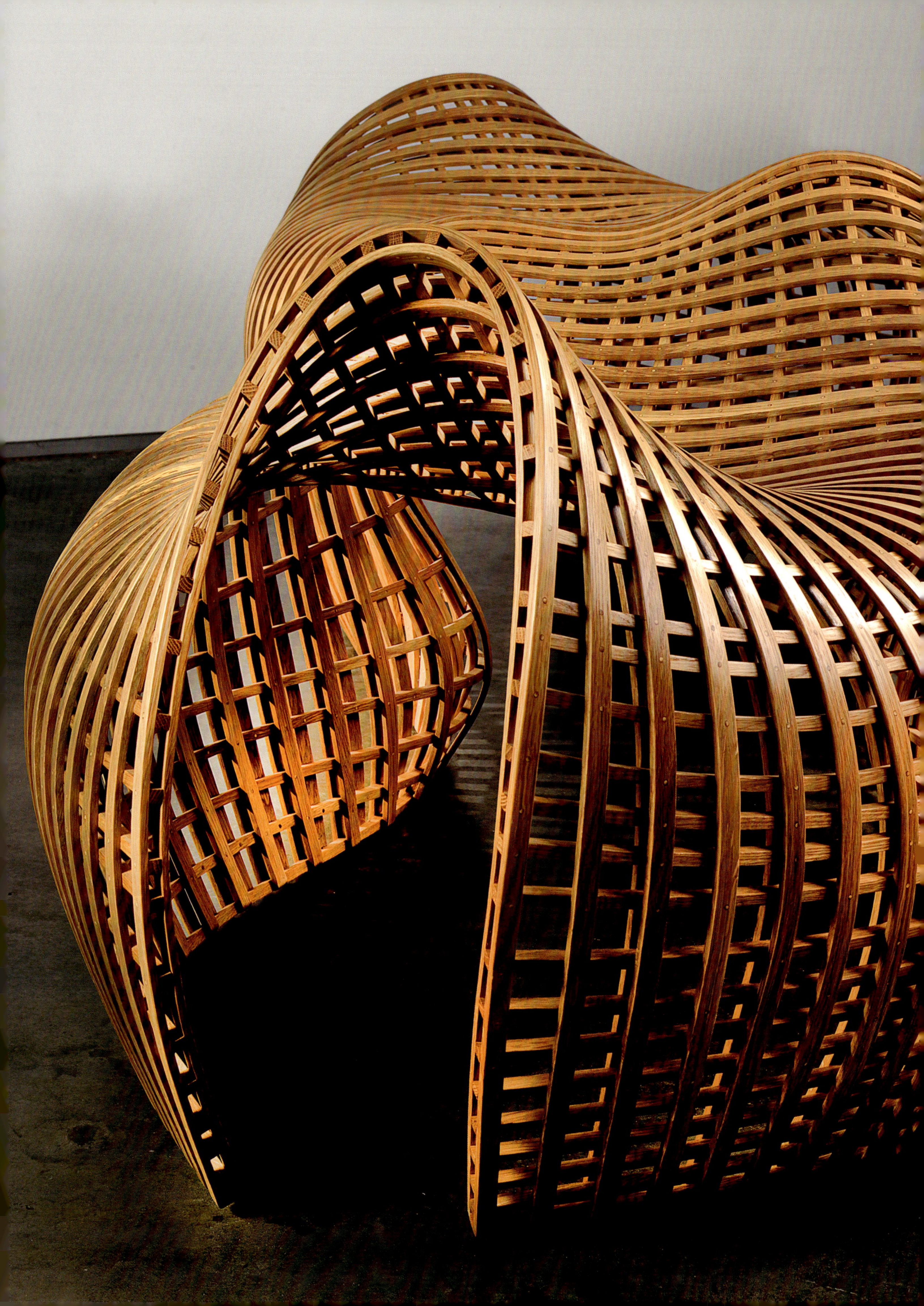

acknowledgments

The Renwick Craft Invitational in its current form would not exist without a generous endowment from the Ryna and Melvin Cohen Family Foundation. The Cohens' gift allows the Renwick to mount a larger exhibition than was originally conceived for this biennial series when it began in 2000, as well as to publish a catalogue, for which the Museum and the American craft community are immensely grateful.

Ulysses Grant Dietz and Andrew Wagner answered my invitation to participate with an enthusiasm that has remained constant through the long process of selecting artists and shepherding the project to fruition. I thank them for their insights into the field, their rigorous conversation, their contributions in print, and for their friendship.

The success of any exhibition involving living artists relies heavily on their cooperation. From the start, Ubaldo Vitali, Cliff Lee, Judith Schaechter, and Matthias Pliessnig have been a joy to work with, not only submitting to lengthy interviews about their work and careers, but also addressing with grace the daily queries and minutiae that make up so much of exhibition business. We are privileged to consider them as integral members of the Renwick's family. We are also grateful to the various institutional and private lenders who parted with their valued collections so that the public could enjoy them in a broad context of the makers' work. Because of them, our wish list of objects remained intact, ensuring a strong representation of the success of these four artists.

A number of individuals offered support in the planning of this year's Invitational. Holly Lee was a gracious host during our visit to Amish country and a frequent source of information on Cliff's work. Louise

Matthias Pliessnig, *Rivulet* (detail), 2009 (see p. 85)

Allison Cort, curator of ceramics at the Smithsonian's Freer Gallery of Art and Arthur M. Sackler Gallery, provided crucial guidance in navigating the complex shoals of Chinese porcelain history. Tom Loeser reminisced about his boat-building sessions at the University of Wisconsin. Lewis Wexler and Sienna Freeman of Wexler Gallery in Philadelphia made contact with each of Pliessnig's lenders and persistently encouraged their involvement in the project. Claire Oliver of Claire Oliver Gallery in New York was equally tenacious in securing Schaechter's most important recent works for the exhibition. Brock Jobe introduced me to Vitali at the artist's Maplewood, New Jersey, studio in 2007. Amber Germano at the Newark Museum aided in bringing important works to Washington. Emily Guthrie located the (uncatalogued!) 1886 Gebrüder Thonet catalogue, proving once again that the answer to every curator's query lies within the Winterthur Library. The James Renwick Alliance and Renato Miracco, cultural attaché at the Embassy of Italy in Washington, DC, organized an impressive slate of programming around the exhibition.

The reality of a museum schedule means that staff at the Renwick and American Art must begin preparations for the next Invitational immediately following the closing of the last. I am deeply indebted to several colleagues for their tireless efforts in realizing this project. In the Publications office, Theresa Slowik, Mary Cleary, and Karen Siatras ensured that this catalogue lived up to its predecessors in terms of quality and content. Photographer Gene Young once again amazed us with his ability to bring diverse media to life on the page. Exhibition designer David Gleeson embraced the challenge of such a varied checklist with characteristic gusto, creating a successful and nuanced installation. Jennifer Lee in the Registrar's office performed the exhausting task of bringing seventy works of every shape, scale, and material to Washington from all points of the country. Fern Bleckner contributed the artists' biographies, while Marguerite Hergesheimer and Rebecca Robinson provided administrative support. Elizabeth Broun, Rachel Allen, Robyn Kennedy, and many others rode with me the roller coaster of small victories that eventually produced this most rewarding of exhibitions.

NRB

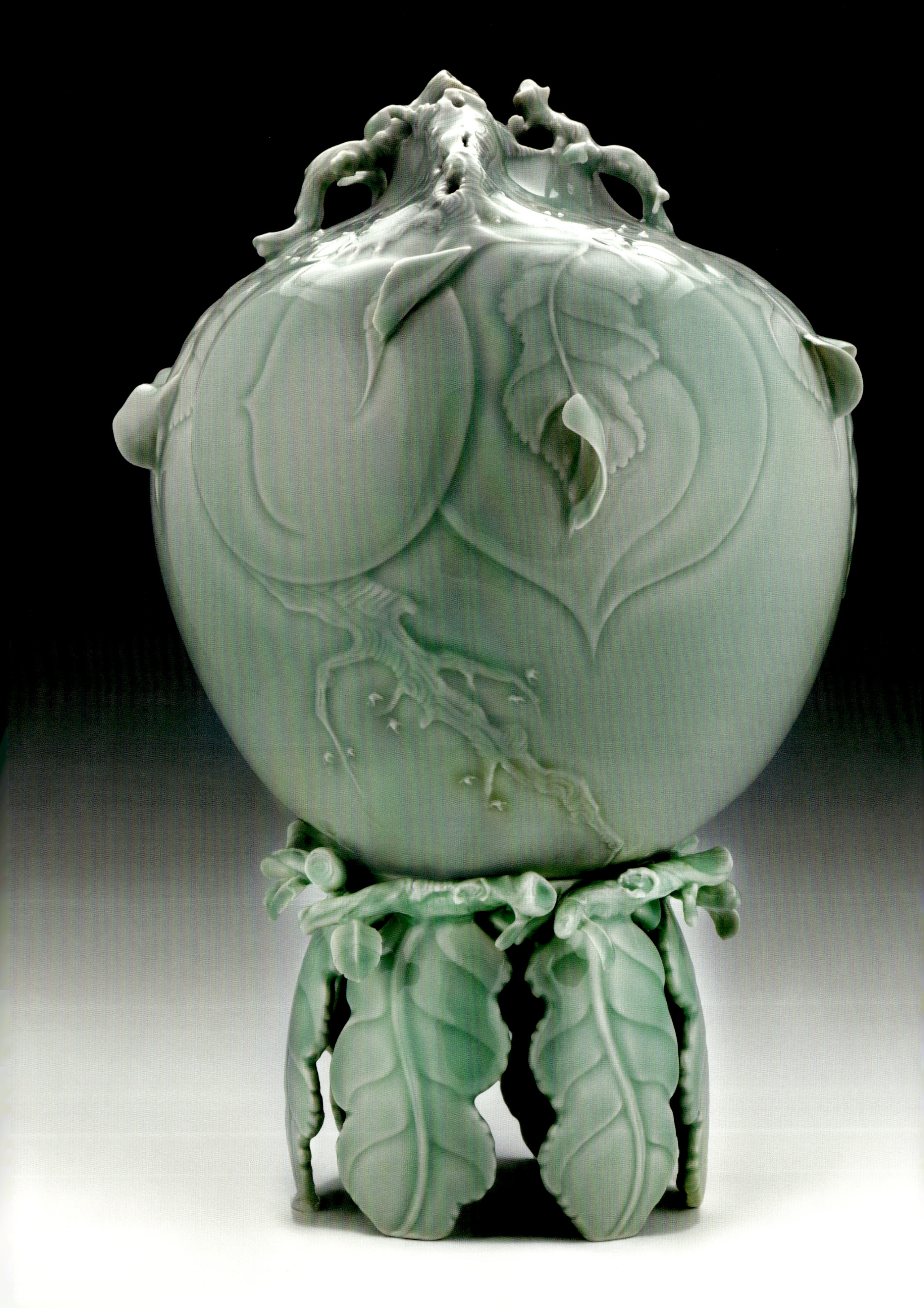

introduction

In the spring of 2009, I asked Ulysses Grant Dietz, senior curator and curator of decorative arts at the Newark Museum, and Andrew Wagner, then editor-in-chief of *American Craft* magazine, to join me in selecting artists for the 2011 Renwick Craft Invitational. In the spirit of this biennial series, each of us drafted a list of artists we considered deserving of wider attention, then met at the Newark Museum for a day of impassioned conversation about artists and broader issues in craft. We quickly realized that several of the names at the top of our lists shared a commonality of inspiration, purpose, and talent in execution. The decision to select Ubaldo Vitali, Cliff Lee, Judith Schaechter, and Matthias Pliessnig for this exhibition was thrilling for reasons evident in the pages that follow.

Contemporary craft holds a necessary and complex relationship with the history of making things. It is at its most fundamental level a reactionary movement rooted in the belief that objects born of individual endeavor hold an intrinsic value otherwise lacking in the mass-produced material culture of the postindustrial age. The act of making something by hand, then, is inherently political, but it is also a means of honoring past practices of skilled work. Raising a clay pot, blowing a glass vessel, weaving cloth, building a chair—all are actions that connect us to the far side of the modern era, during which there was little reason to distinguish between modes of production. Even if they are not familiar with specific technical or aesthetic histories, most craft artists are mindful that centuries of precedent hum beneath the surface of their work.

The four artists selected for this exhibition differ in that they are *acutely* aware of contemporary craft's antecedents and employ their

Cliff Lee, *Peach,* 2005, porcelain and celadon glaze. Collection of the artist

depth of knowledge in the creation of their respective oeuvres. This is not to say that their work is derivative or nostalgic—rather, Vitali, Lee, Schaechter, and Pliessnig use diverse histories of craftsmanship and creative expression as points of departure in the pursuit of original art.

Ubaldo Vitali (b. 1944) is a fourth-generation silversmith, trained in the guild system of Rome, whose Old World education ties him directly to the practices of generations that have come before him. He is also a master conservator of antique silver and draws on his grasp of historical techniques to shape the contemporary pieces for which he is best known. Cliff Lee (b. 1951) was raised in Taiwan, surrounded by China's rich ceramic past. His career as a neurosurgeon was eventually overshadowed by his passion for clay, and he uses his skilled hands to mold and carve impeccable vessels in homemade porcelain. His understanding of chemistry has also proven invaluable as a basis for re-creating previously lost Chinese glazes. Judith Schaechter (b. 1961) finds inspiration for her stained glass windows across a broad spectrum, including allegorical paintings, medieval tapestries, the political history of church windows, and the American Civil War. She deftly blends these disparate ingredients into a postmodern stew of content, uniquely identifiable to the artist, who has almost single-handedly resurrected the art of stained glass in American studio craft. Matthias Pliessnig (b. 1978) uses traditional boat-building techniques to construct extraordinary amorphous furniture. Their organic forms are designed with 3-D modeling software, then assembled from steam-bent strips of white oak, melding ancient and futuristic technologies in the pursuit of comfort.

This exhibition demonstrates the continuing pull of function as a subject of investigation in American craft. While some pieces are made for use and others are not, each artist's work addresses this base rationale for manufacture. They are scaled to our bodies so that we may hold them (Vitali and Lee), or that they may hold us (Pliessnig) or shelter us (Schaechter). Their allure is in the visceral response they induce and in the evidence of the maker's touch: always on the surface, always at hand.

In drawing from cultural histories on three continents, and from the diversity of their experiences—begun in four separate decades—the artists in this exhibition also highlight the depth of the creative wellspring for contemporary craft in the United States. The objects herein reassure that a world chock-full of stuff cannot limit the passion or skill of the most dedicated individuals to produce works of uncommon splendor.

NICHOLAS R. BELL
Curator
Renwick Gallery of the Smithsonian American Art Museum

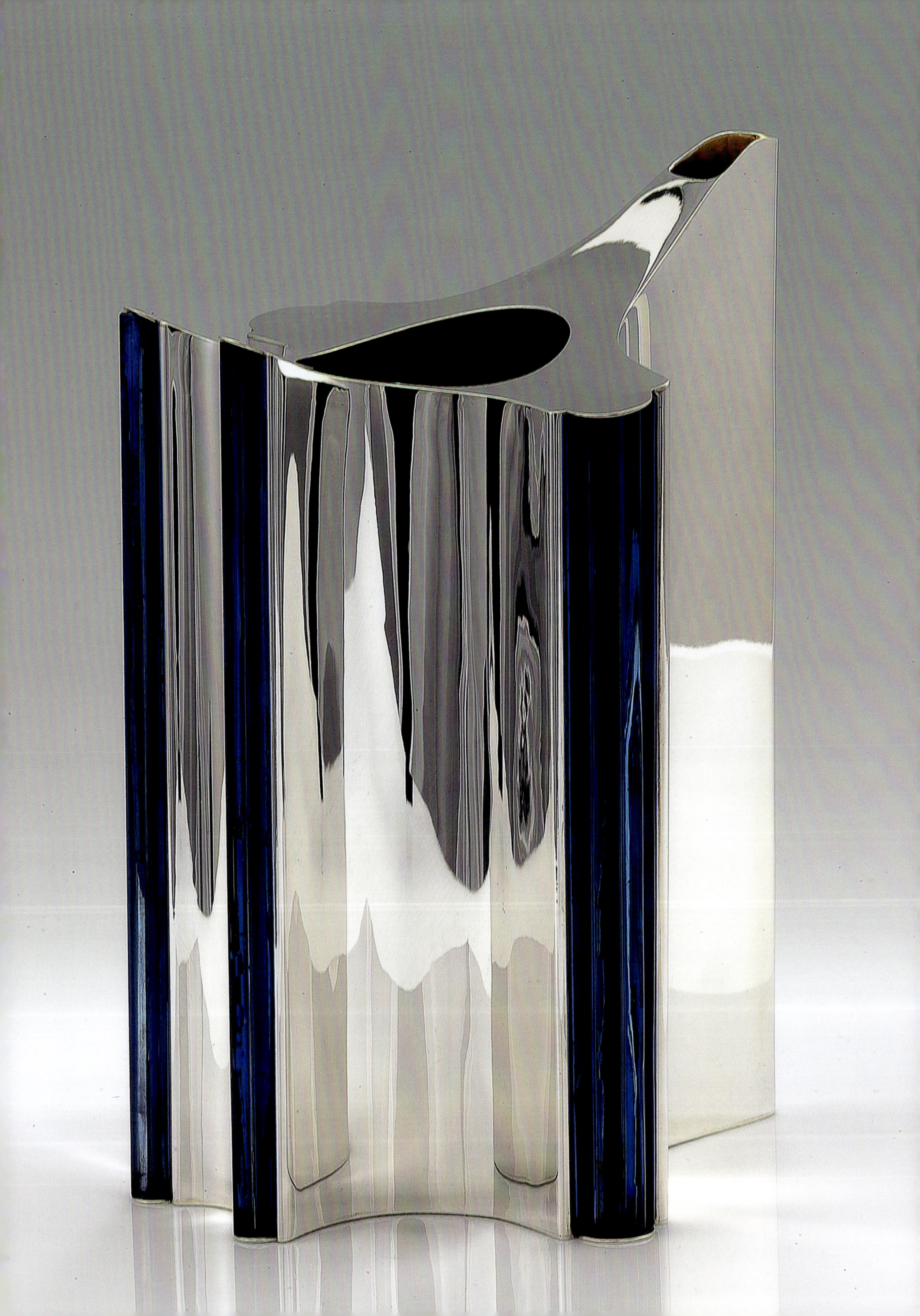

ubaldo vitali

Ubaldo Vitali is, arguably, the greatest living silversmith in the United States. An artist and artisan, he is—by his own definition—an alchemist. The popular myth of alchemy, with its images of quasi-magical types and stone-walled rooms dimmed by sulphurous vapors, focuses on the transformation of lead into gold. But for Ubaldo Vitali, it has a more nuanced meaning. His alchemy is the transformation of a material (silver) into a work of art, transcending the mechanics of craftsmanship by reaching the very soul of the metal. Making a silver object is as much a spiritual as a physical transformation.

Ubaldo Vitali was born in 1944 and raised and educated in his native Rome. He studied art history, architecture, sculpting, and painting at the Liceo Artistico Ripetta, Accademia di Belle Arti, and the Università di

***"Baroque Church" Pitcher,* 1989, silver and glass. Collection of the artist**

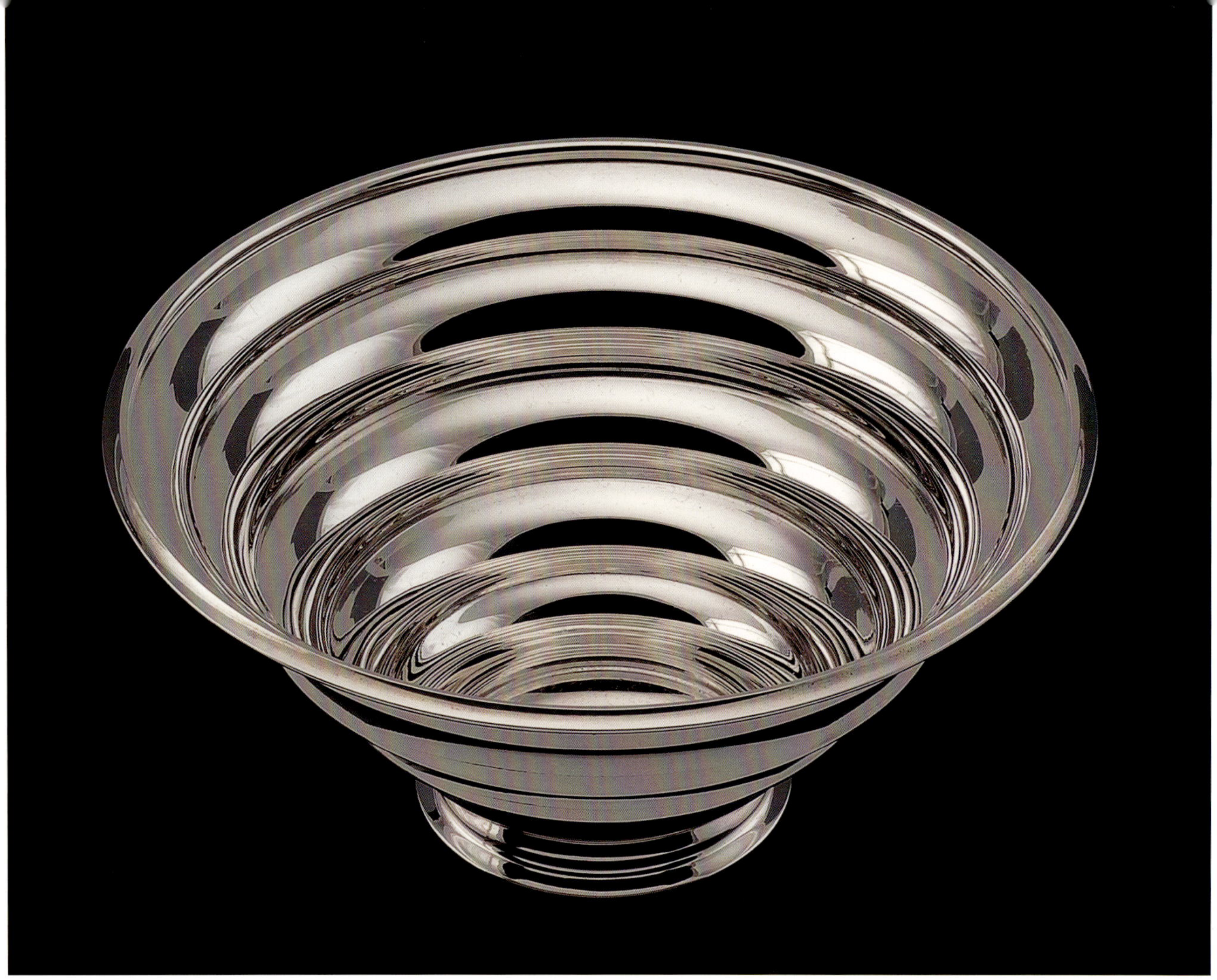

Fig. 1
***Ribbed Conical Bowl,* 1976, silver. Collection of the artist**

Fig. 2
***Cup,* 1980, silver and gilding. Collection of the Newark Museum, Gift of the artist, 1984, 84.10**

Roma in the 1960s, and as a student won awards for his painting. Forty years later, he is still an active member of the Università e Nobil Collegio degli Orefici Argentieri dell'Alma Città di Roma, the Roman goldsmith's guild whose origins date back to the Renaissance. Vitali is the guild's only member allowed to reside outside Rome. His great-grandfather and namesake founded a silversmith shop in Rome in 1886. Vitali's expertise in antique silver has strongly influenced his own modernist style, because it has enabled him to understand both the physical structure of antique silver objects and the intellectual process behind their design and production.

Vitali came to Newark, New Jersey, in 1967, where his bride-to-be's family lived. He established a studio in Belleville near the Tiffany & Co. silver factory, later moving to a workshop in the nearby suburb of Maplewood. During the 1970s and 1980s, he did extensive work for

Tiffany, along with producing and designing objects for other high-end retailers such as Bulgari, Cartier, and Steuben. Over the course of his career he has received commissions for presentation pieces for three popes, the former shah of Iran, Queen Elizabeth II, and Presidents Lyndon Johnson, Richard Nixon, and Ronald Reagan. That he is not better known in the contemporary craft world is partly owed to the particular trajectory of his career.

His earliest work for luxury retailers produced, for the most part, small-scale objects of the sort that would appeal to affluent nesters. A sleek ribbed bowl designed for Cartier appealed to the revived interest in art deco design in the 1970s (fig. 1). An iconic Dixie Cup designed for Bulgari in the late 1970s was simultaneously a sly jet-set toy and a small-scale Claes Oldenburg sculpture that was also functional (fig. 2). Having mastered the art of lost-wax casting, which was a crucial element in the development of rococo silver in eighteenth-century Europe, Vitali remodeled stock "grand tour" objects for Tiffany in the 1970s, creating modern *objets de luxe* that enjoy an enduring popularity. His *singerie* candleholders, inspired by eighteenth-century prototypes, are better made than their European originals;[1] and the crab-and-urchin candlestick, cast from nature, offers a fresh take on both rococo naturalism and Victorian Japanism through his expert eyes (fig. 3).[2]

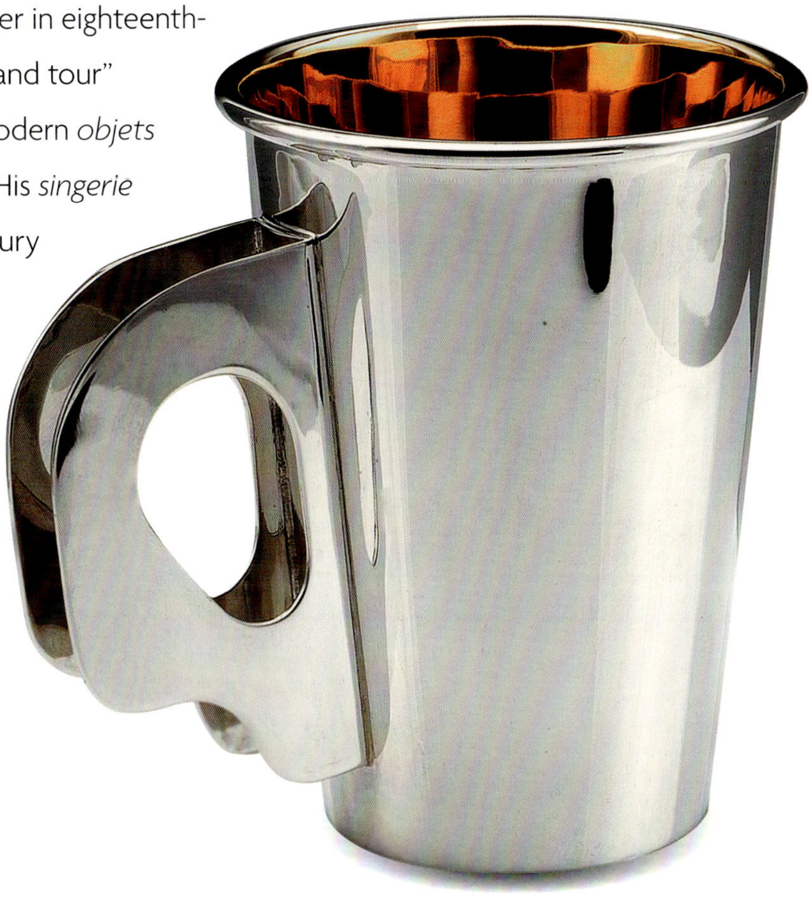

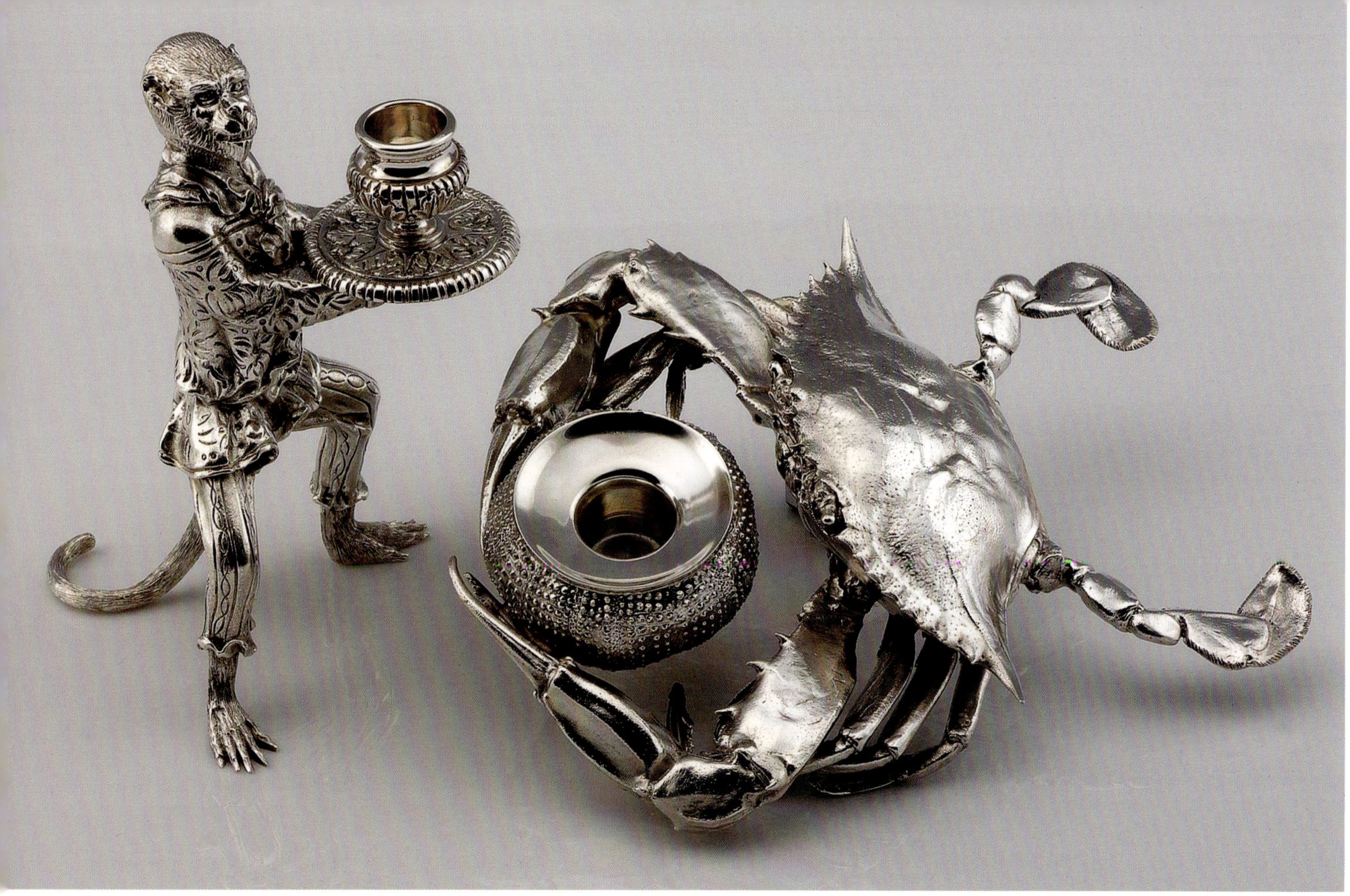

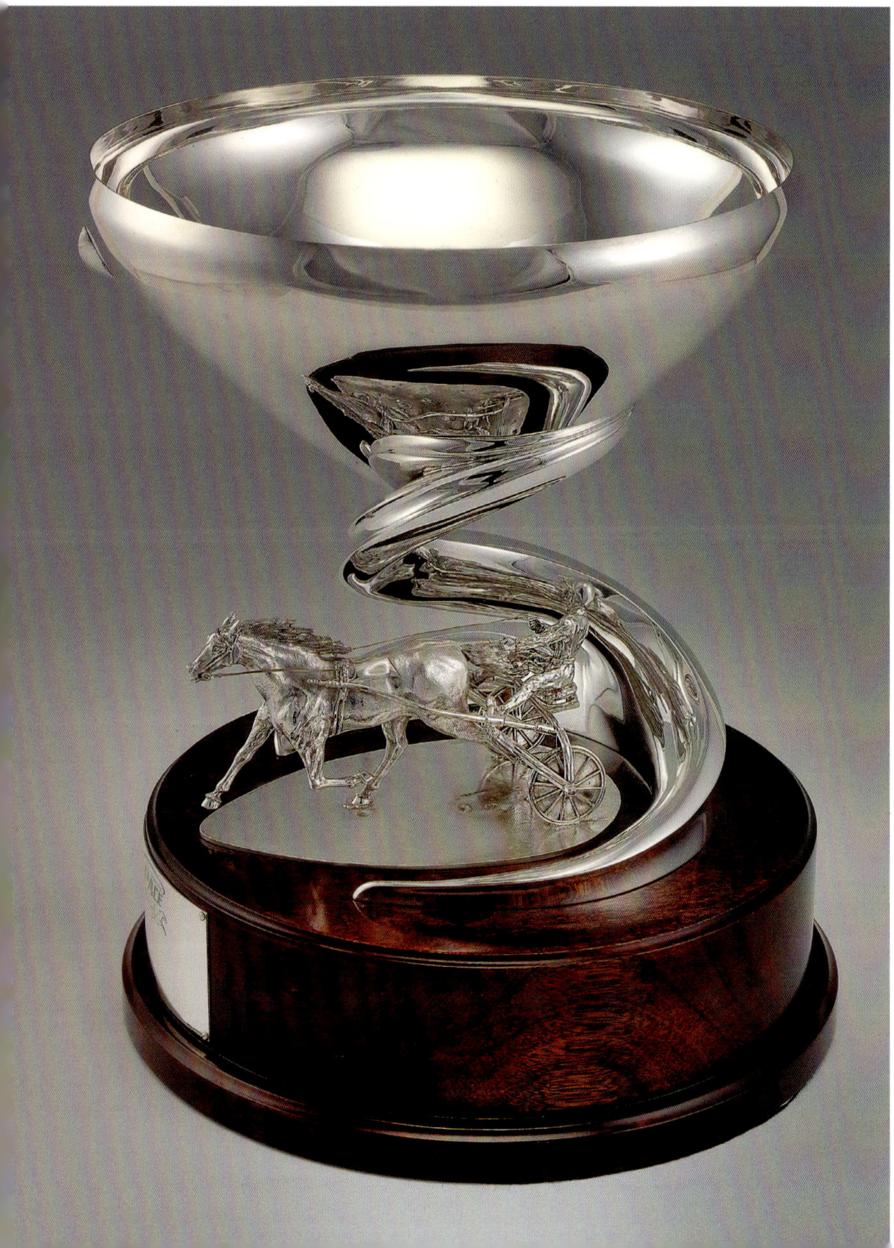

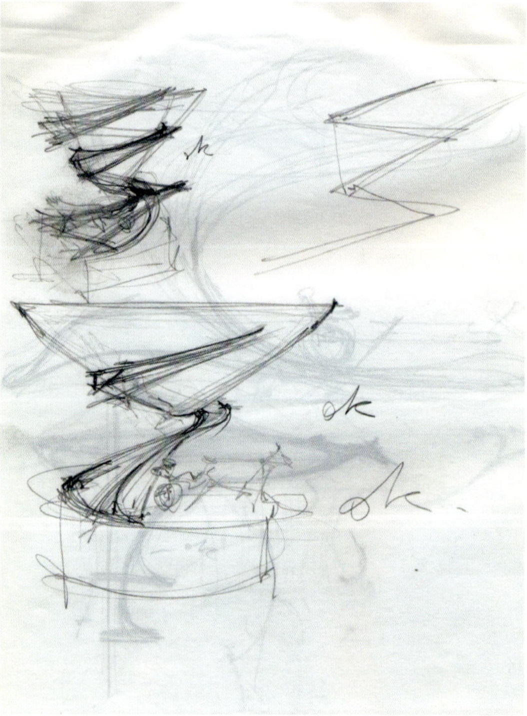

Another important aspect of Vitali's career in America has been the production of sports trophies, which calls on his skills as a silversmith and as a sculptor. For several years he executed the Meadowlands Pace Trophy for harness racing, based on the traditional trophy formula consisting of a reproduction eighteenth-century English cup with a cast horse as decoration. In 1998, he was asked to design a new Pace Trophy for the twenty-fifth anniversary of the race (figs. 4, 5). Vitali's design features a sweeping tornado-like vessel raised by hand from sheet silver, anchored by a finely detailed cast figure of a pacing horse with its sulky jockey. It combines sleek modernist design with highly detailed traditional process, capturing the movement and excitement of the event.

Because of his remarkable range of silversmithing skills—at a time when the number of gifted American silversmiths was on the wane—Vitali quickly developed a substantial practice as a conservator of important historical silver. He has for several decades been the silversmith of choice for complex or delicate work brought to him by museums, private collectors, and auction houses from around the world. Simultaneously, he has developed an international reputation as a scholar on both the aesthetics and the making of great silver, exploring the intersection of art and craft over the centuries.[3] When the New-York Historical Society needed a unique colonial teapot conserved, it was entrusted to Vitali's shop (fig. 6). The late seventeenth-century pear-shaped teapot by Kiliaen van Rensselaer, with its lush baroque coat of arms, had lost its handle and one of the handle sockets. It had various dents and old cracks filled with lead solder (a silversmith's nemesis, as

Fig. 3
Singerie Candlestick, **about 1976, silver. Collection of the artist**

Crab and Urchin Candlestick, **about 1976, silver. Collection of the artist**

Fig. 4
The Meadowlands Pace Trophy, **2000, silver and wood. Collection of the artist**

Fig. 5
Sketch for *The Meadowlands Pace Trophy,* **2000, paper vellum. Collection of the artist**

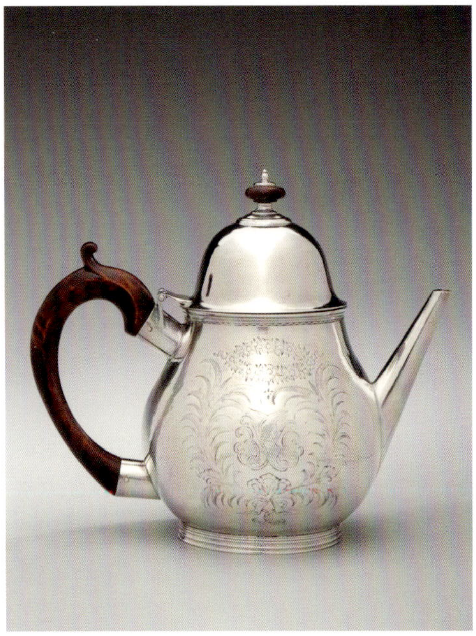

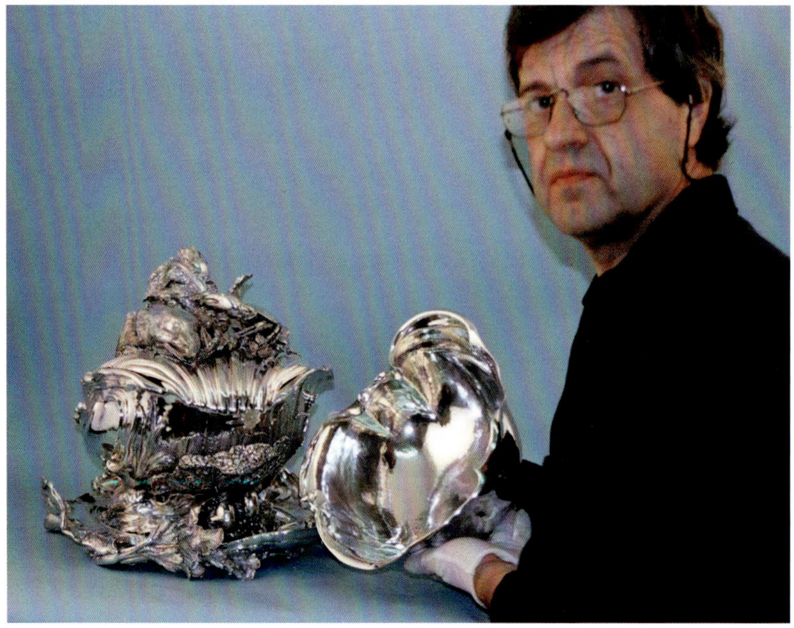

Fig. 6
Kiliaen van Rensselaer (1663–1719), *Teapot*, about 1683–95, silver and wood. Collection of the New-York Historical Society, Bequest of Major Philip Schuyler, 1915.20

Fig. 7
Ubaldo Vitali with the new liner for the Meissonnier tureen

lead has a damaging effect on silver over time). And in 1998, when Sotheby's auction house sold an astonishing rococo soup tureen designed in the late 1730s for the English duke of Kingston by the French silversmith Juste-Aurèle Meissonnier (1695–1750), Vitali was asked to work on it. He not only conserved and repaired the inherent weaknesses of a complex cast object more than 250 years old, but upon request he also designed a replacement for its long-lost silver liner, so that the new owner could use the tureen (fig. 7).[4]

The interrelationship of the arts is central to Vitali's craft. He considers every project, whether a large-scale trophy or a small water pitcher, a sculpture. Production pieces for retailers are as carefully crafted as unique objects made for museums. "It doesn't matter if it's a coffeepot or a cathedral; both must be sensitive to construction and interaction with space."[5] That approach is seen vividly in a water pitcher trimmed with Venetian glass that Vitali designed and produced for Bulgari in the 1980s (see page 20). He started with a footprint that evoked the architectural plan of an Italian baroque church. The cruciform cross section is disguised by the upswept handle and spout, as well as by the vertical lines of blue glass.

For a tea and coffee service commissioned by the Newark Museum to mark its seventy-fifth anniversary in 1984, the footprint was inspired by the idea of a polygonal tent, its canvas stretched between vertical poles and pulled into taut wings by invisible ropes (fig. 8). For this project, Vitali was charged with creating a modern interpretation of a Victorian concept—the silver tea and coffee service, which had become the centerpiece of the affluent American parlor by the middle of the nineteenth century. Vitali translated the key elements—teapot, coffeepot, sugar, creamer, and tray—into a sculptural assemblage unified by both materials (silver, trimmed with ebony and ivory) and sweeping concavities that fracture and redistribute light. Although not intended for use, the set had to be functional—it had to work and feel balanced in the hand. The kidney-bean-shaped openings of the handles on each piece contrast with the straight verticals of the outside edges of the handles but also provide a comfortable grip. The sculpted ebony handles also serve the same practical function as they do on antique silver: to insulate the hand from the highly conductive metal.

A complex, intuitive geometry is central to Vitali's designs. He often begins with pencil sketches, covering pages of computer printer paper with quickly rendered ideas, most of which never move beyond the embryonic stage (fig. 9). For a tureen designed for a private collector in Chicago, Vitali created sketches that helped him visualize angles and curves, to anticipate the spatial relationship among the various parts (fig. 10). The result was an undulating, shimmering form, the baroque roots of which are readily discernible (fig. 11). Inspired by the wavelike forms in

(following pages)

Fig. 8
Coffee and Tea Service,
1983–84, silver, ebony, ivory, and Plexiglas. Collection of the Newark Museum, Purchase 1984 The Members' Fund, 84.1

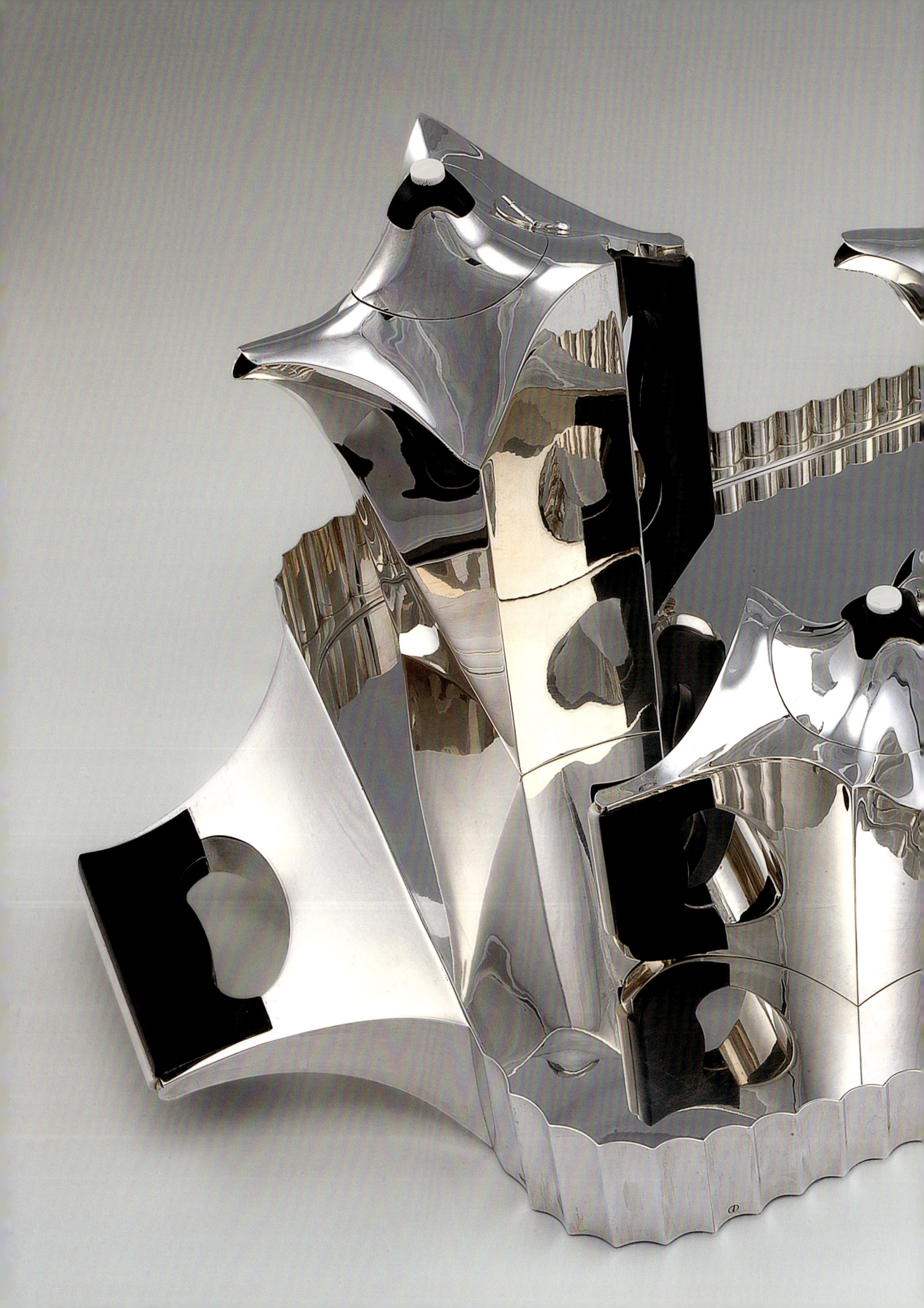

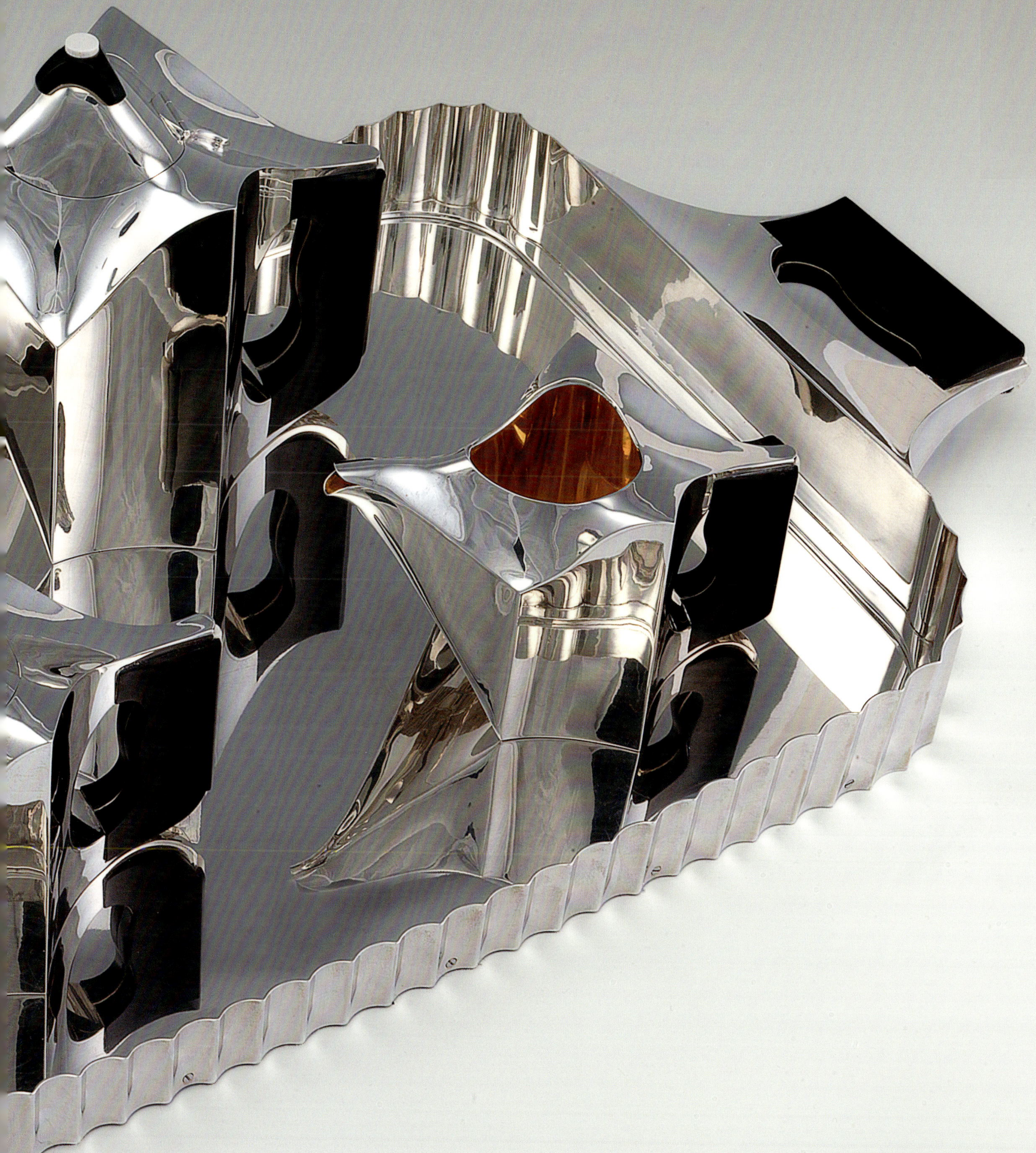

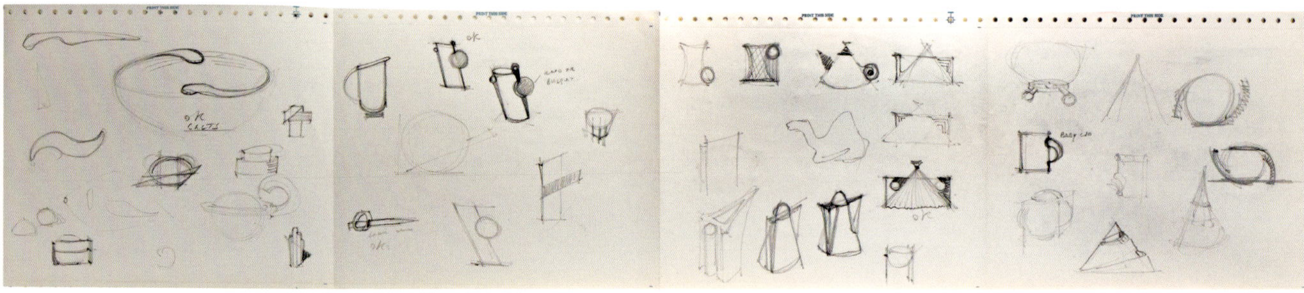

Fig. 9
Doodles and sketches, 1990s, paper. Collection of the artist

(opposite, clockwise from lower left)

Fig. 10
Sketch for *Tureen*, 1980s, paper. Collection of Dr. John Batzel

Fig. 11
***Tureen*, 2001, silver and sodalite. Collection of the artist**

Fig. 12
***Covered Tureen with Stand*, 1989–90, sterling silver and ebony. The Museum of Fine Arts, Houston, Museum purchase with funds provided by the National Endowment for the Arts, with gifts of the Interior Resource Center, William J. Hill and John G. Middleton, 90.372.a–c**

the design, Vitali incorporated deep-sea-blue sodalite in the handles and added ornament in the form of sea creatures, cast from life in the eighteenth-century manner.[6] Although a bit closer in feeling to the rococo masterworks he has conserved, this tureen remains a work of modern art and craft. A second version of this tureen was commissioned by the Museum of Fine Arts, Houston, without the cast ornaments and using ebony for the handles, which emphasize its sleek modernity (fig. 12). When the Houston tureen was first exhibited, the gallery lights created reflections on the adjacent walls closely echoing his original drawings.[7] In spite of his skills in casting and chasing, Vitali generally reserves these methods for his conservation work and only rarely uses them to ornament his modernist designs. "I play with light and reflections instead of those little details," he says. "That's my rebellion."[8]

In 1986, Vitali designed one of his most monumental works for a commission in Texas (fig. 13). As with the Newark service, it was intended to evoke an antique form, in this case an epergne, an elaborate dining-room centerpiece that combines candleholders with containers for fruit or flowers. The design of the centerpiece also recalls the latent symbolism that much aristocratic European silver incorporated during the eighteenth century. At first glance the assembled elements seem entirely abstract, but a subtle iconography emerges on closer inspection. The upswept candlesticks of silver and ivory-pale maple hold suspended on their pinnacles a central bowl in the form of a five-pointed star. In between the candlesticks are five biomorphic dishes with undulating outlines that rise up to meet at a point just below the slumped midpoint of the

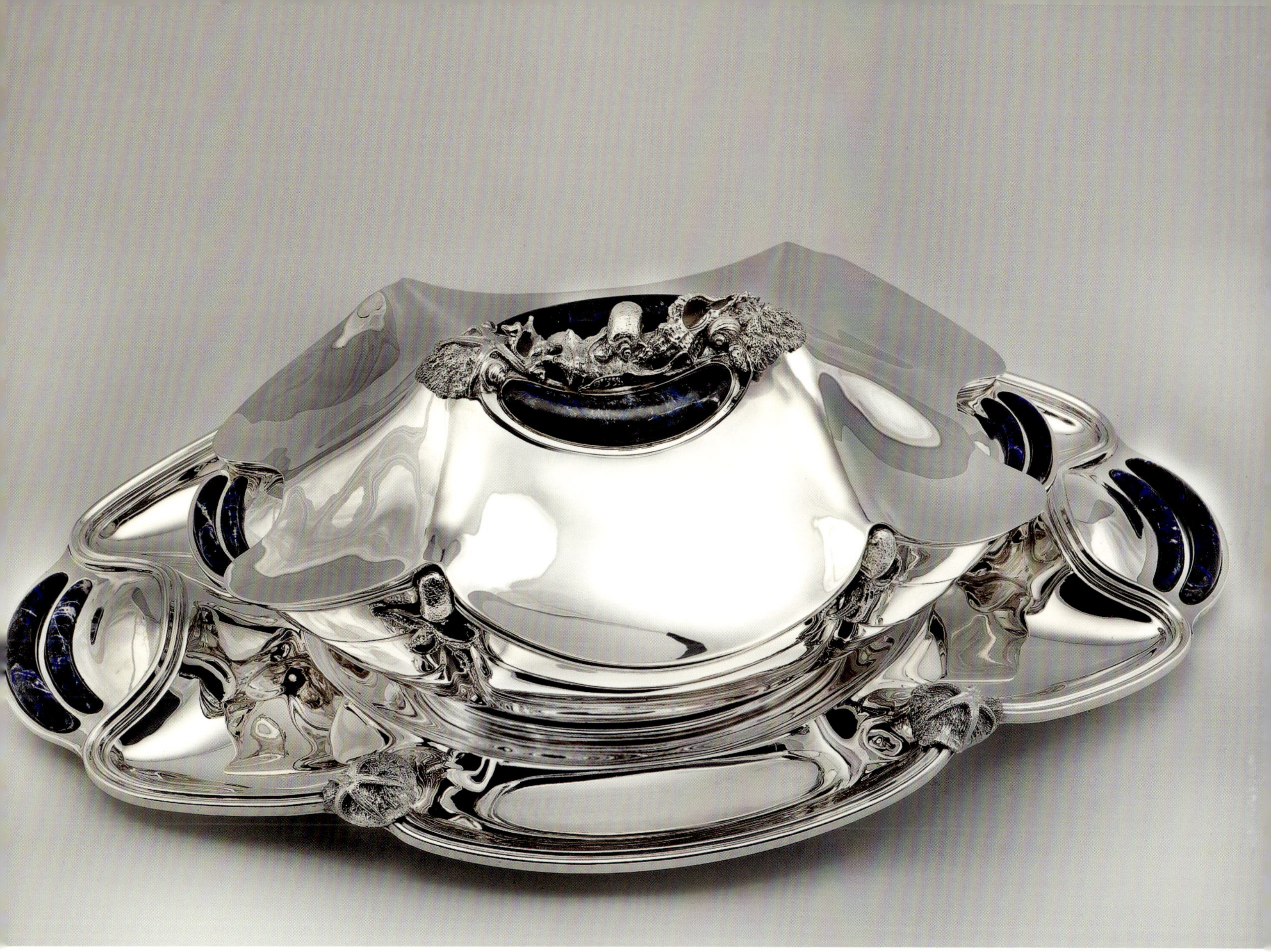

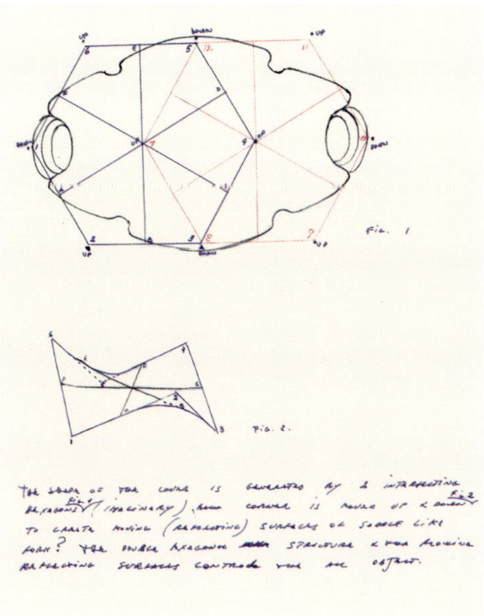

UP
DOWN
Fig. 1
Fig. 2.
THE SHAPE OF THE COVER IS GENERATED BY 2 INTERSECTING HEXAGONS (IMAGINARY), EACH CORNER IS MOVED UP & DOWN
TO CREATE MOVING (REFLECTING) SURFACES OR SADDLE LIKE FORM? THE DOUBLE HEXAGONAL STRUCTURE & THE MOVING REFLECTING SURFACES CONTROLS THE OBJECT.

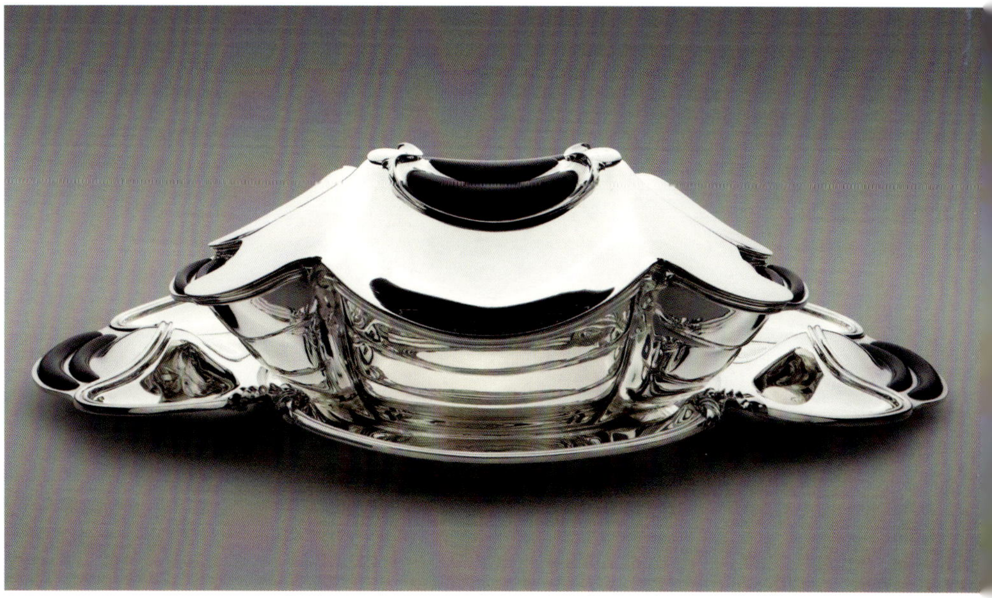

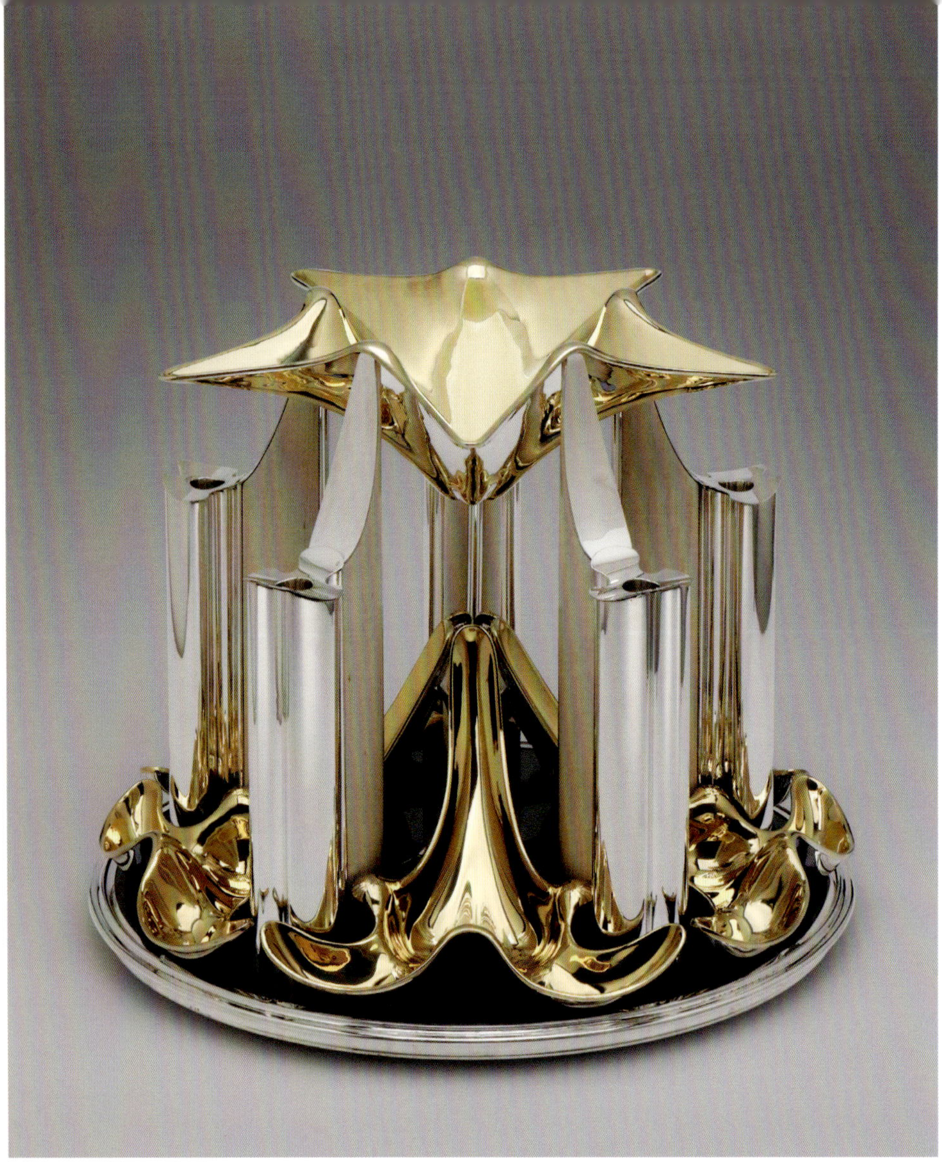

Fig. 13
Centerpiece, 1986, sterling silver, silver gilt, bleached maple, and glass. Collection of the Yale University Art Gallery, Janet and Simeon Braguin Fund, 2007.181.1

Fig. 14
50th Anniversary Centerpiece, 1994, silver and glass. Collection of Mrs. Iris Schwartz

central star. These can be seen as stylized longhorn skulls, although a certain intentional phallic quality underlies both these dishes and the footprint of the candleholders. The smoked glass lining the circular tray may represent the oil from which Texas derives its legendary wealth.

The Texas epergne was followed by another ambitious centerpiece, commissioned by two New Jersey silver collectors to commemorate their fiftieth wedding anniversary (fig. 14).[9] This epergne offered no covert symbolism, but instead paid homage to the burgeoning interest in the art nouveau style, with its sinuous, organic forms. Vitali incorporated custom-made Venetian glass—as he did with some of his designs for Bulgari—adding an element of light and color to this piece, which breaks down into two smaller centerpiece components.

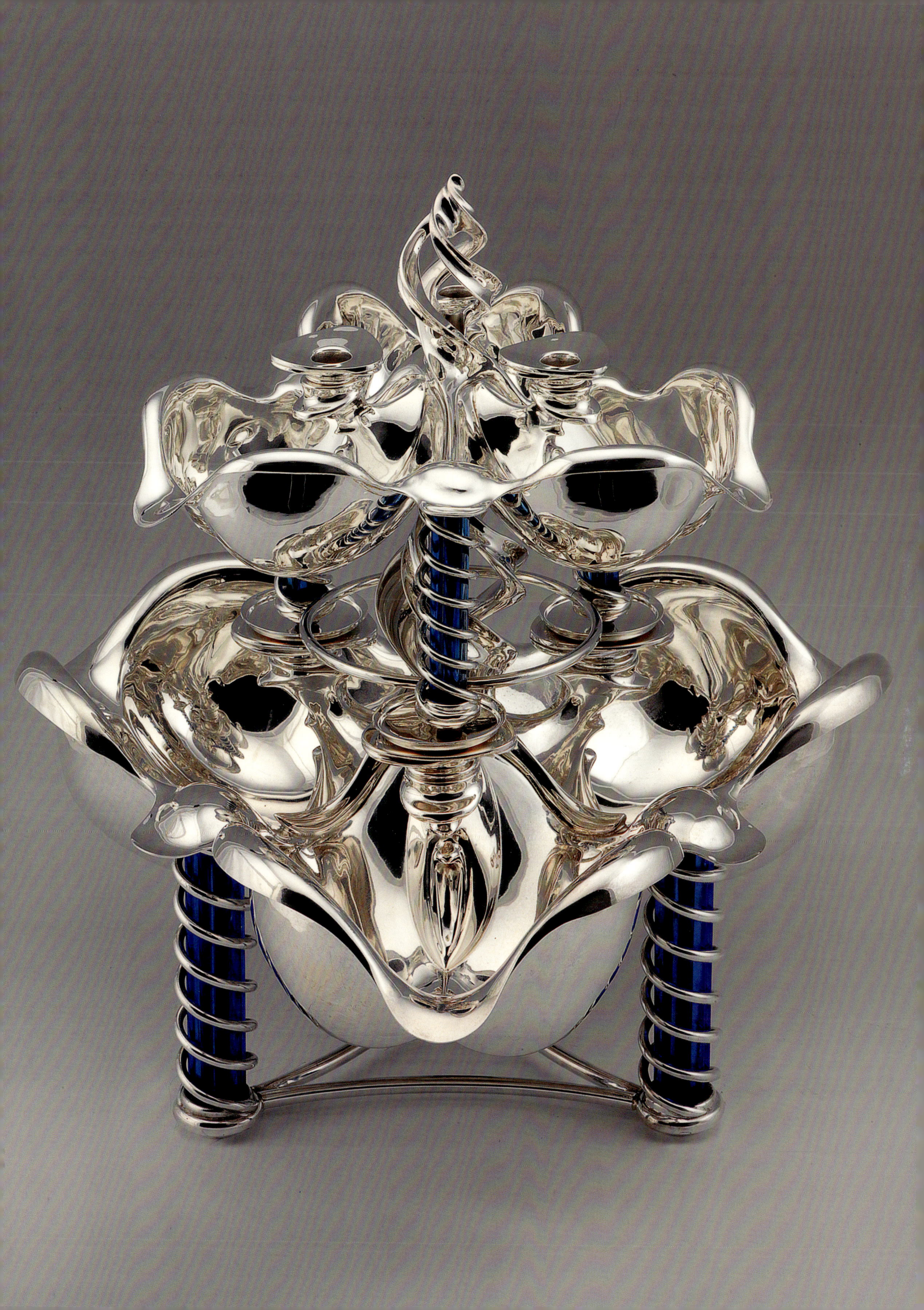

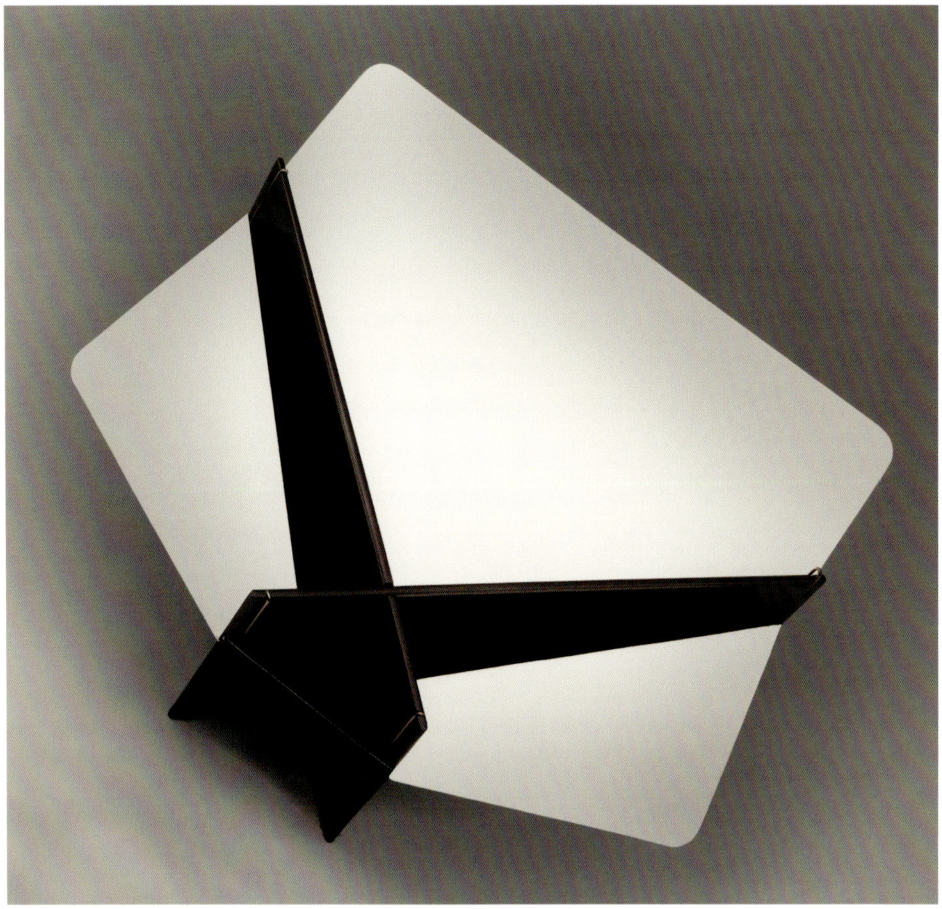
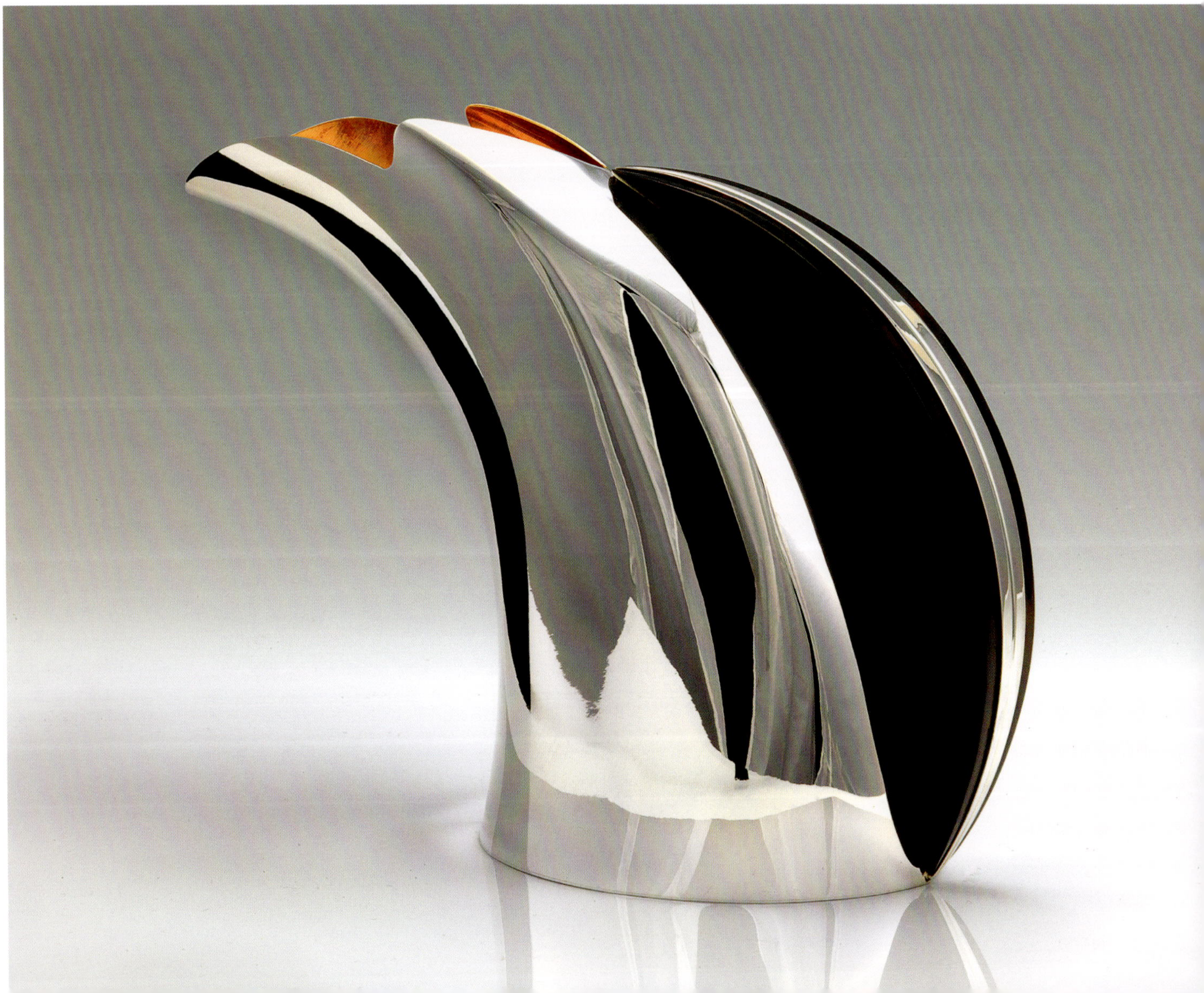

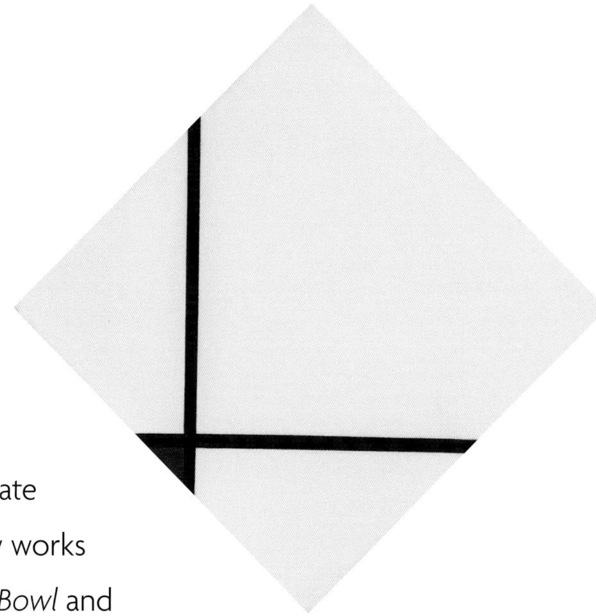

Throughout Vitali's career, the mixing of materials has intrigued him for both aesthetic and structural reasons. In the late 1990s, working initially with Movado, he created a series of new works using wood and glass in combination with silver. His *Mondrian Bowl* and *Triple Wave Pitcher* use ebony in strikingly different ways (figs. 15, 16). While the bowl takes the mathematical grid of a Piet Mondrian painting (fig. 17) as a footprint and pulls it into three dimensions, the pitcher is organic and sensual, the traditional materials seamlessly sculpted into a completely modern (and perfectly balanced) object. It was through the Movado commission that Vitali joined forces with a New Jersey glass artist, Leonard DiNardo, to produce a group of objects that were both sculptural and functional. A two-light candelabrum and a coffee service designed by Vitali, with cased-glass elements made by DiNardo, reflect the postmodern aesthetic in their stripped-down, classicizing geometry and bright, jewel-like colors (figs. 18, 19).[10]

Today, more than forty years after he arrived in the United States, Ubaldo Vitali is still a busy man. His workshop overflows with scores of handmade tools accumulated over a lifetime, each with its own place on the walls or workbench. A large open hearth fills one side of the room—something he built a few years ago as part of a project to re-create medieval aquamanilia from the Metropolitan Museum of Art's collection for an exhibition at the Bard Graduate Center in New York.[11] These Old World touches are balanced by the latest equipment and technology necessary for today's scientific and conservation processes. In this workshop he gives demonstrations, teaches, and continues to design and

Fig. 15
***Mondrian Bowl,* 1999, patinated bronze and silver plate. Collection of the artist**

Fig. 16
***Triple Wave Pitcher,* 1999, silver and ebony. Collection of the artist**

Fig. 17
Piet Mondrian (1872–1944), *Composition with Blue,* 1926, oil on canvas, 24 1/16 × 24 1/16 in. Philadelphia Museum of Art, A. E. Gallatin Collection, 1952, 1952-61-87

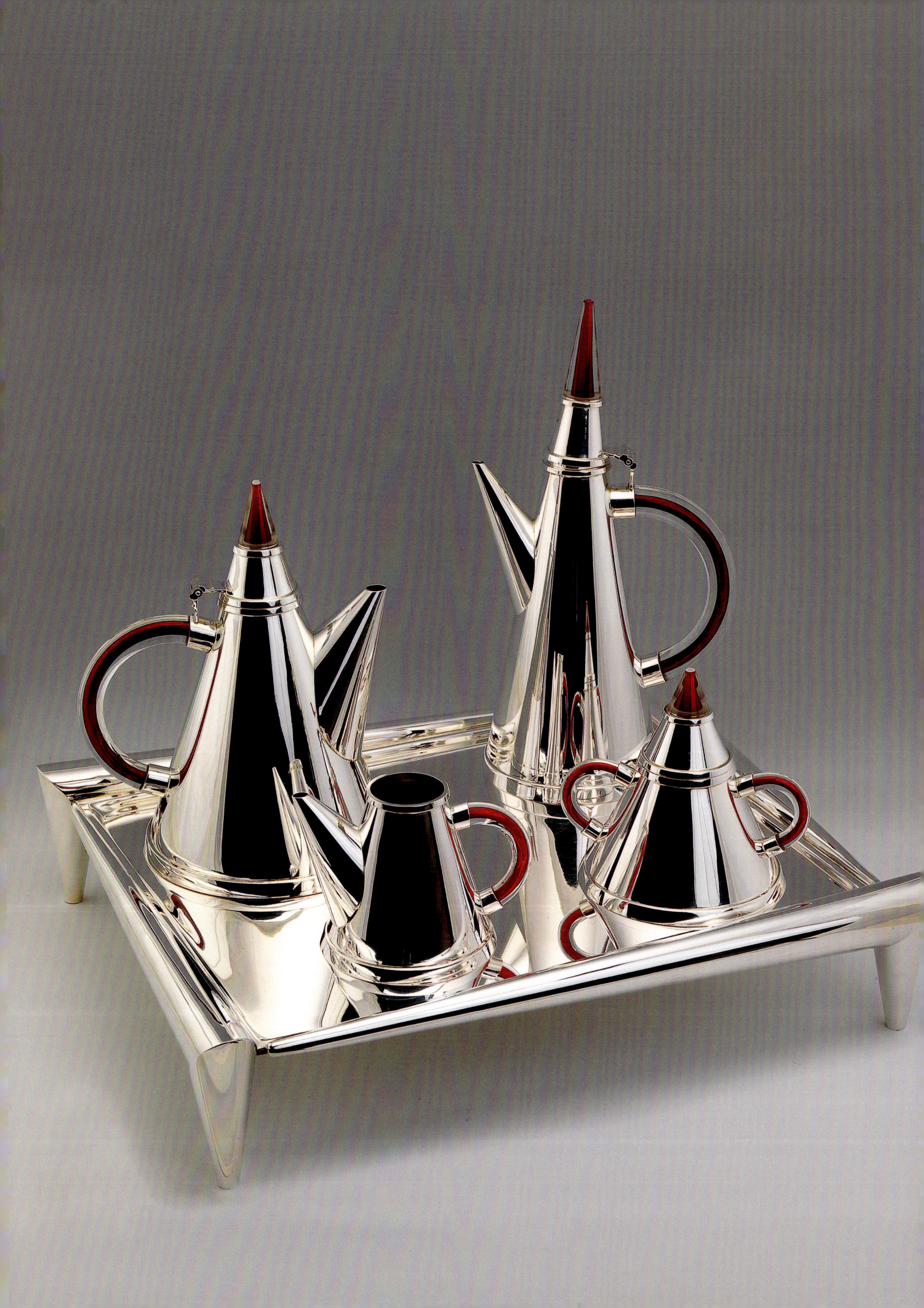

make objects that are the best of their kind in the world. He depends on his shop assistants, without whom he could not do what he does. Foremost among them are Anthony Cavaleri, who has worked with Vitali for more than thirty years, and Amrit Tamrakar, a fourth-generation silversmith from Katmandu, Nepal, who has worked in the studio for more than a decade. Vitali is revered by an international coterie who know his work and are awed by his skill. While he regrets what he sees as the decline—globally—of the art of silversmithing, he has no regrets about the path he chose decades ago when, as a teenager in Italy, he first picked up a hammer and put a piece of silver on the anvil. In Ubaldo Vitali's gifted hands, past and present form a remarkable continuum.

ULYSSES GRANT DIETZ

Fig. 18
***25th Anniversary Tea and Coffee Service*, 2004 (designed in 1999), silver and glass (glass by Leonard DiNardo). Collection of Janet and Ricardo Zapata**

Fig. 19
***T-form Two-Light Candelabrum*, 1999, silver and glass. Collection of the artist**

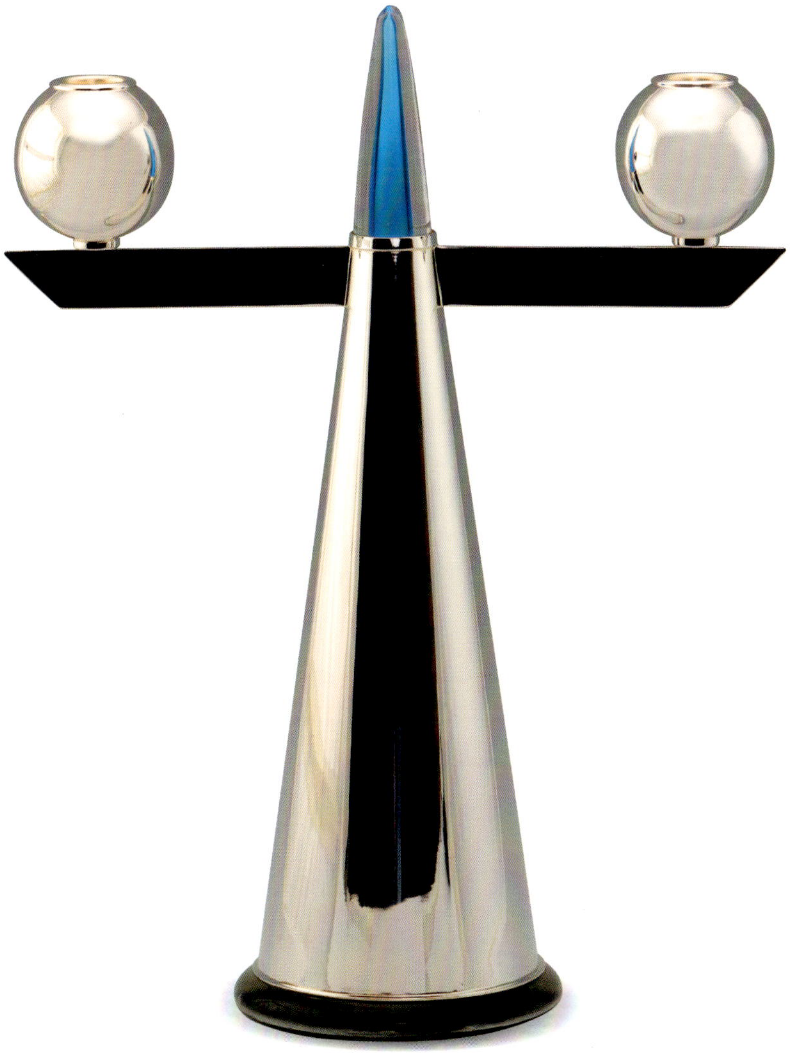

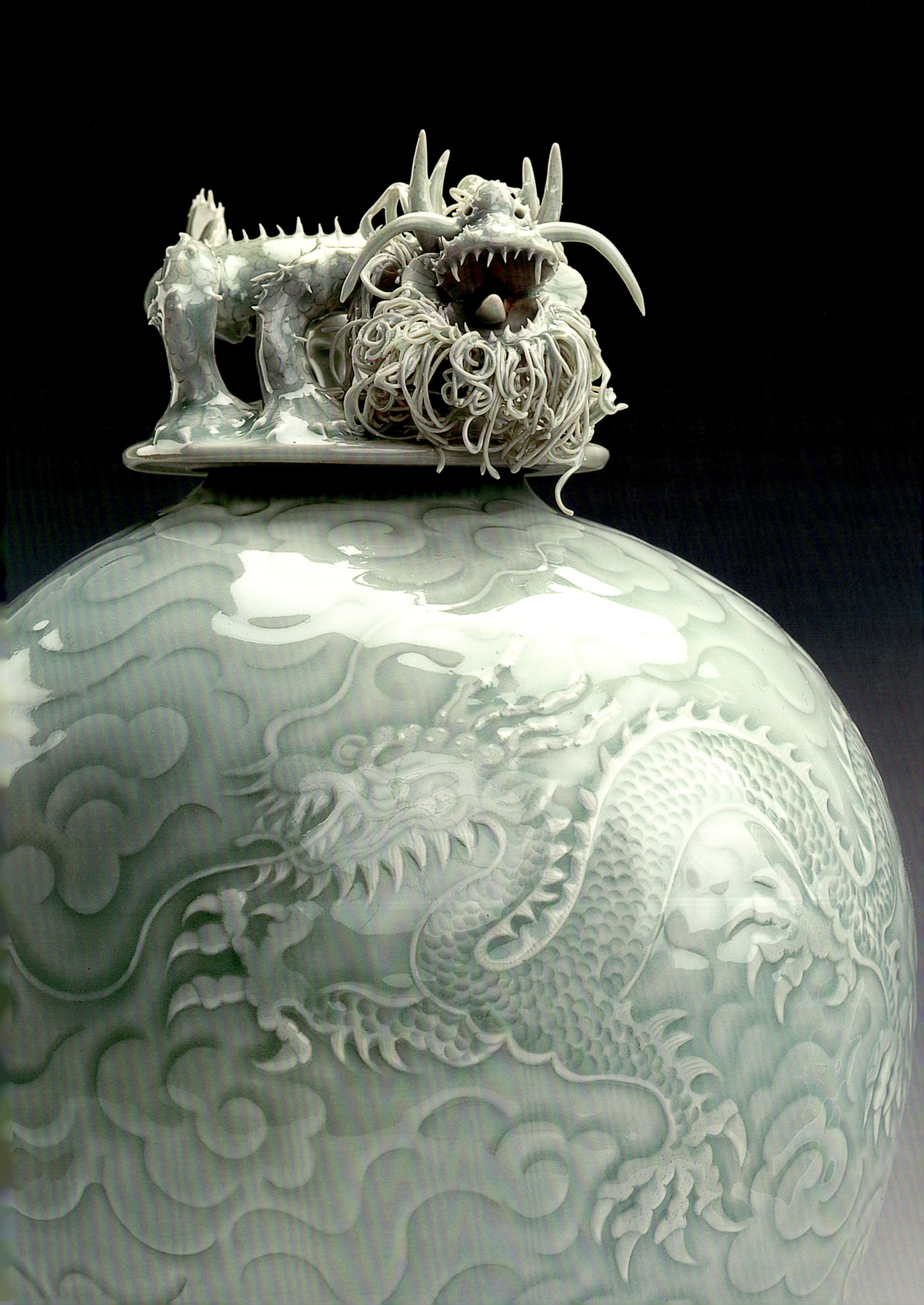

cliff lee

Chinese porcelain has beguiled the West for centuries, its pure white, vitreous quality inspiring a long history of emulation, both aesthetic and eventually material, with the discovery of kaolin in Europe and the United States. That history largely dominated American interest in Asian ceramics until the mid-twentieth century, when the teachings of Soetsu Yanagi, Bernard Leach, and others introduced the *mingei* philosophy, whose celebration of the utilitarian and the value of imperfection elicited a craze for Japanese style and stoneware ceramics.

A number of American studio potters continue working in porcelain, although the majority employ its unique qualities to highly individualized ends, best illustrated in the 1980 Renwick exhibition *American Porcelain: New Expressions in an Ancient Art.* Only a handful, including Catharine

***Double Dragon on Cloud Pedestal* (detail), 2009 (see p. 44)**

Hiersoux, Janel Jacobson, Adrian Saxe, and more recently Steven Young Lee, have explored the rarified clay's aesthetic roots south of the Yangtze River. Cliff Lee belongs to this small cadre, yet stands alone in his sensitivity to the source and the intensity with which he channels China's ceramic past into contemporary American work.

Lee is particularly well suited to bridge tradition and innovation in clay. Raised in Taiwan, the son of a diplomat in Chiang Kai-shek's Nationalist government, he was surrounded by examples of Chinese porcelain both at home and the frequently visited National Palace Museum, and steeped in the dynastic history that forms the basic narrative for the region's arts. He attended university and medical school in the United States, then practiced neurosurgery in Pennsylvania for five years before stress drove him in search of an avocation. After a patient introduced him to the medium, Lee attended ceramics courses at Virginia's James Madison University, and was instantly hooked by the potter's wheel and its ability to block the distractions of the outside world.

Lee's formal education in the field was marked by a thirst for technical knowledge and a wary eye toward the funk aesthetic that dominated American ceramics in the 1970s—two early traits that provide insight into his mature work. Students in the program were not encouraged to mix their own clay or glazes or to fire their work, steps Lee recognized as crucial to a solid foundation in the medium. He compensated in part by volunteering to staff the kiln, firing the work of the entire class while gaining valuable experience. He also set about stripping his (then stoneware) vessels of excess clay, developing sparse new forms weighted

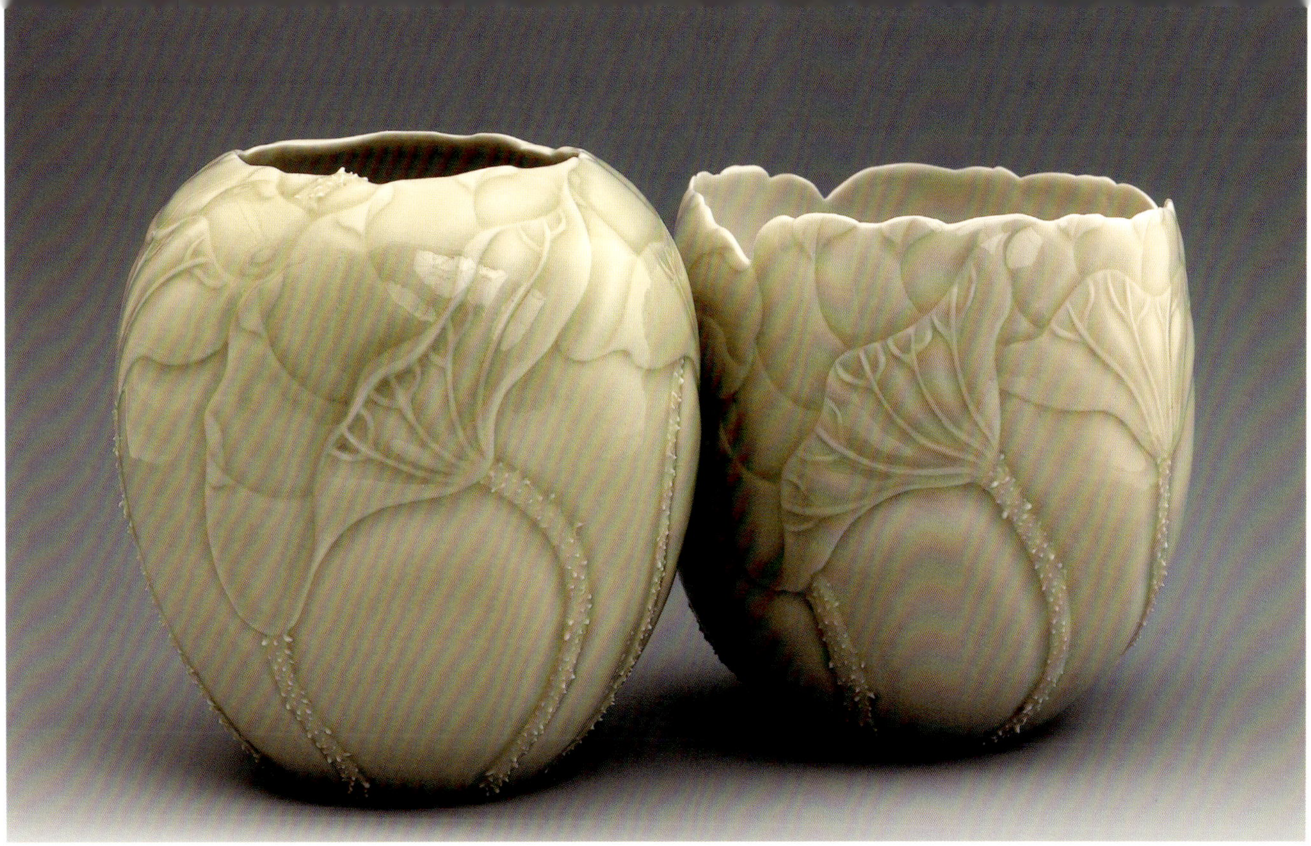

toward function rather than ornament. Lee completed his MFA over the course of two sabbaticals and then returned briefly to his medical practice. The degree to which ceramics now captivated him was quickly revealed when he noted (dangerously, he thought) the similarities between a patient's skull and a clay pot. It was a sign to move on.

Fig. 20
***Lotus Bowls*, 2000, porcelain and ivory celadon glaze. Collection of the artist**

The extraordinary body of work Cliff Lee has produced over the last three decades hinges on the complementary relationship between his Taiwanese upbringing, the technical knowledge acquired through practicing medicine, and the agility and perfectionism demanded of a surgeon. Soon after leaving his practice, Lee switched clays precisely for the challenge posed by what he calls an "honest material."[12] Rather than hide behind stoneware's ability to mask minor flaws with its longer and darker grain, Lee embraced the naked quality of porcelain and its tendency to highlight any speck of dirt or small dimple. "I hate impurities," says Lee, a fact borne out by the pristine walls of his vessels (fig. 20). To exert the quality control necessary to meet this standard, Lee mixes his own porcelain from kaolin, feldspar, and silica, ensuring he is the only middleman between raw earth and the final work. To increase the

Fig. 21
***Lotus Vase with Flower,* 2009, porcelain and celadon glaze. Collection of the artist**

porcelain's notoriously low elasticity, Lee forms the clay into pucks that rest for up to a year.

The switch to porcelain was followed in the late 1980s by a shift away from production work (a comfortable medium for the novice), toward pieces that emphasize contemplation over function (fig. 21). It was a change that allowed Lee not only to focus attention on the integrity of his materials, but also to raise increasingly thinner-walled vessels, revealing porcelain's famed translucence. The ability to control light as it filters through the clay is made possible by Lee's exquisite carving, which typically integrates decoration with a vessel's structure, thereby avoiding the excessive use of material anathema to the artist. Using scalpels and homemade tools, Lee deftly cuts into the soft walls of his unfired pots, permitting the edge of each subject to glow. Protrusions such as thorns, stamens, and whiskers are painstakingly applied with needles and tweezers. Lotus flowers, koi, dragonflies, and fruit trees surrounding the Lees' rural property in Lancaster County, Pennsylvania, offer inspiration, while dragons symbolize good luck in Chinese culture (fig. 22; see also p. 38).

Lee's dexterity in carving can be attributed to his surgical experience, but his grasp of content draws from a much deeper source than his backyard. He studied the carved ivory and porcelain collections of several East Coast museums, including the Smithsonian's Freer Gallery of Art, where he would have seen examples similar to this Yuan dynasty (1271–1368) bottle with intricate vinescrolls (fig. 23); the decoration is primarily molded, then carved for added effect, in keeping with the technique of the period.[13] The translucent-blue *qingbai* glaze on this bottle,

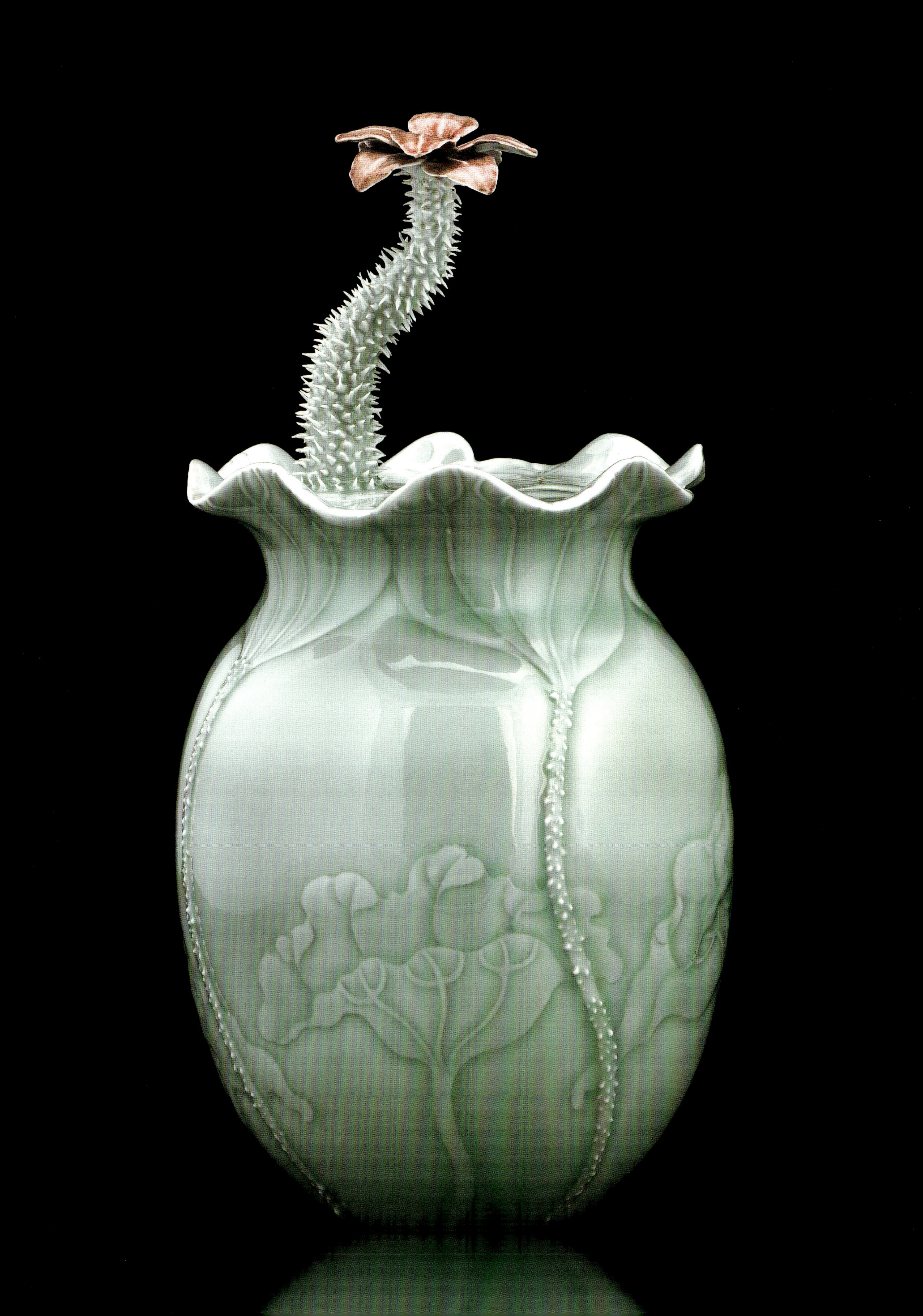

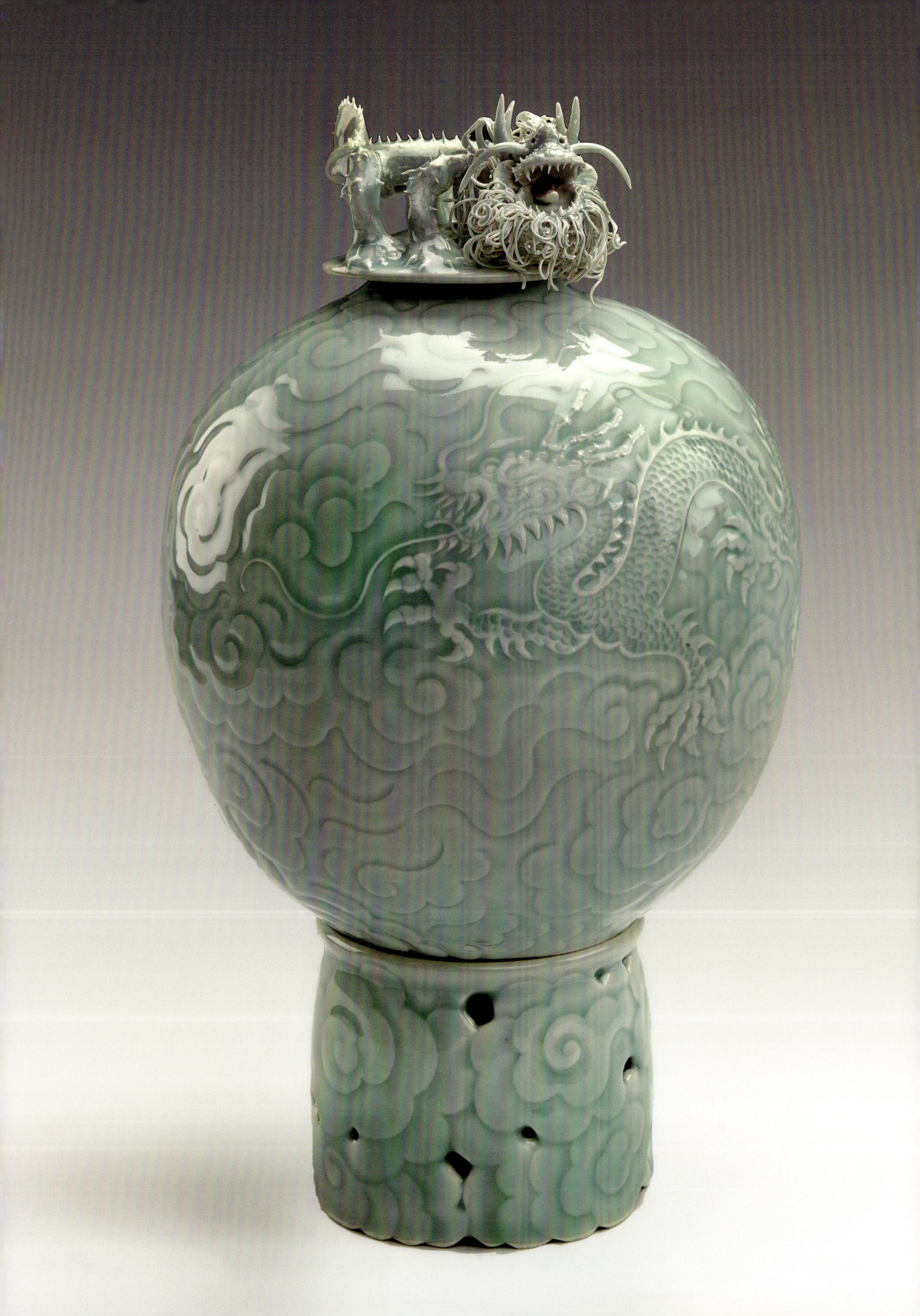

introduced in the Jingdezhen region during the influential Song dynasty (960–1279), pools perfectly among the scrolls, adding depth and color to the design. It is an effect long sought after in the West, achieved both historically and by Lee through the control of trace iron oxide levels in the glaze (commercial glazes typically lack this depth). Lee acquiesces to modern parlance in calling his pale green glaze "celadon," a moniker this color is thought to have acquired through the green-clothed protagonist of the same name in Honoré d'Urfé's seventeenth-century novel *L'Astrée*.[14] True celadon ranges (with increasing iron levels) from olive green to blue-green and is thickly applied to stoneware more often than to porcelain.

While celadon is now the most widely recognized monochromatic Chinese glaze (if only in name), it is only one of several other glazes developed through the Yuan, Ming (1368–1644), and Qing (1644–1911) dynasties, the dramatic hues of which continue to resonate in Lee's work. To reproduce them with both visual and compositional accuracy, Lee has spent years researching the chemical makeup of particular glazes. Circumstantial evidence such as where a potter (if known) was born and trained, where the kiln site was located, and what minerals were likely present given its geographic location, is often the most helpful. Trial and error, hunches, and Lee's training in chemistry all play a role in the sometimes quixotic quest to re-create glaze effects often lost to history (fig. 24). The moment of truth, as for all potters, arrives with the opening of the kiln door after the second firing. Weeks, if not months, of effort can amount to little except disappointment, due both to glaze failures and the 50 percent loss rate owed to Lee's discerning eye.

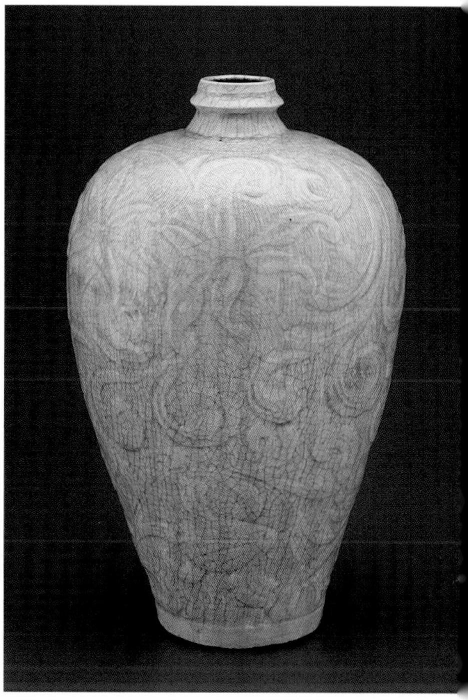

Fig. 22
***Double Dragon on Cloud Pedestal*, 2009, porcelain, celadon glaze, and rubies. Collection of the artist**

Fig. 23
Unidentified artist, *Bottle of Meiping Form*, 13th–14th century, porcelain with translucent bluish *(qingbai)* glaze, 14 ¾ × 9 ⅛ in. Freer Gallery of Art, Smithsonian Institution, Washington, DC, Gift of Charles Lang Freer, F1897.58

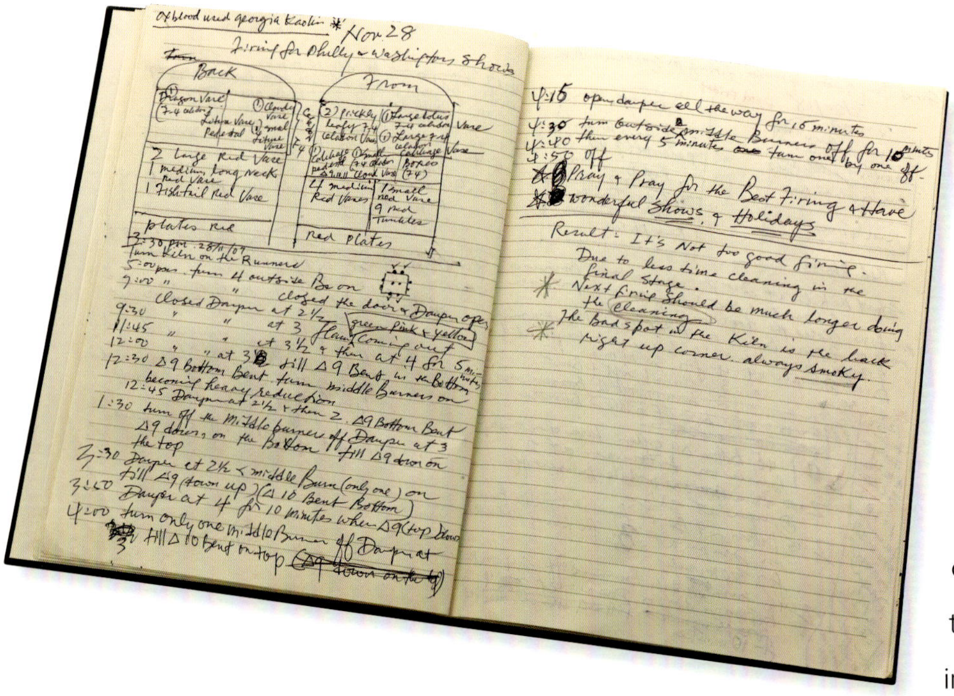

Then there are the small miracles that make his efforts worthwhile. After seventeen years of trying, Lee was able to replicate the famed and ever-fleeting imperial yellow glaze, so called for the exclusive position it enjoyed in the Ming court from its introduction in the fifteenth century (figs. 25, 26). The egg yolk, or "chicken fat," coloration of the lead silicate-based enamel glaze has eluded many a pretender for centuries, and was immediately lost again to Lee for three years, demonstrating its elusive appeal and prompting the artist to recount an oft-told (and apocryphal) tale of Chinese potters literally losing their heads over their failures to reproduce it.[15]

Fig. 24
Pages from Lee's kiln notebook, 2005–10, bound paper. Collection of the artist

Fig. 25
***Prickly Melons*, 2008, porcelain and imperial yellow glaze. Collection of the artist**

Fig. 26
***Anniversary Tea Set*, 2001, porcelain, imperial yellow glaze, and silver (silver handle by Holly Lee). Collection of Dr. Todd and Lisa Hoover**

Similarly challenging to create with any consistency are copper-red glazes such as oxblood, and the lighter peach bloom, which is believed to have been discovered accidentally during the early Qing dynasty (figs. 27, 28).[16] Peach bloom's mottled pink with specks of moss green, blue, or purple appears only during a short window in reduction firing, requiring both diligence and luck on the part of the maker. The precious quality of this particular example is enhanced by its survival through the firing process, despite the glaze's having sealed the opening at its stem.

Copper's inclination to dance around the kiln during firing is illustrated in the pink blush on a large *guan*-ware teardrop and vase (fig. 29). *Guan* ware, a type of celadon, was introduced as the official ware of

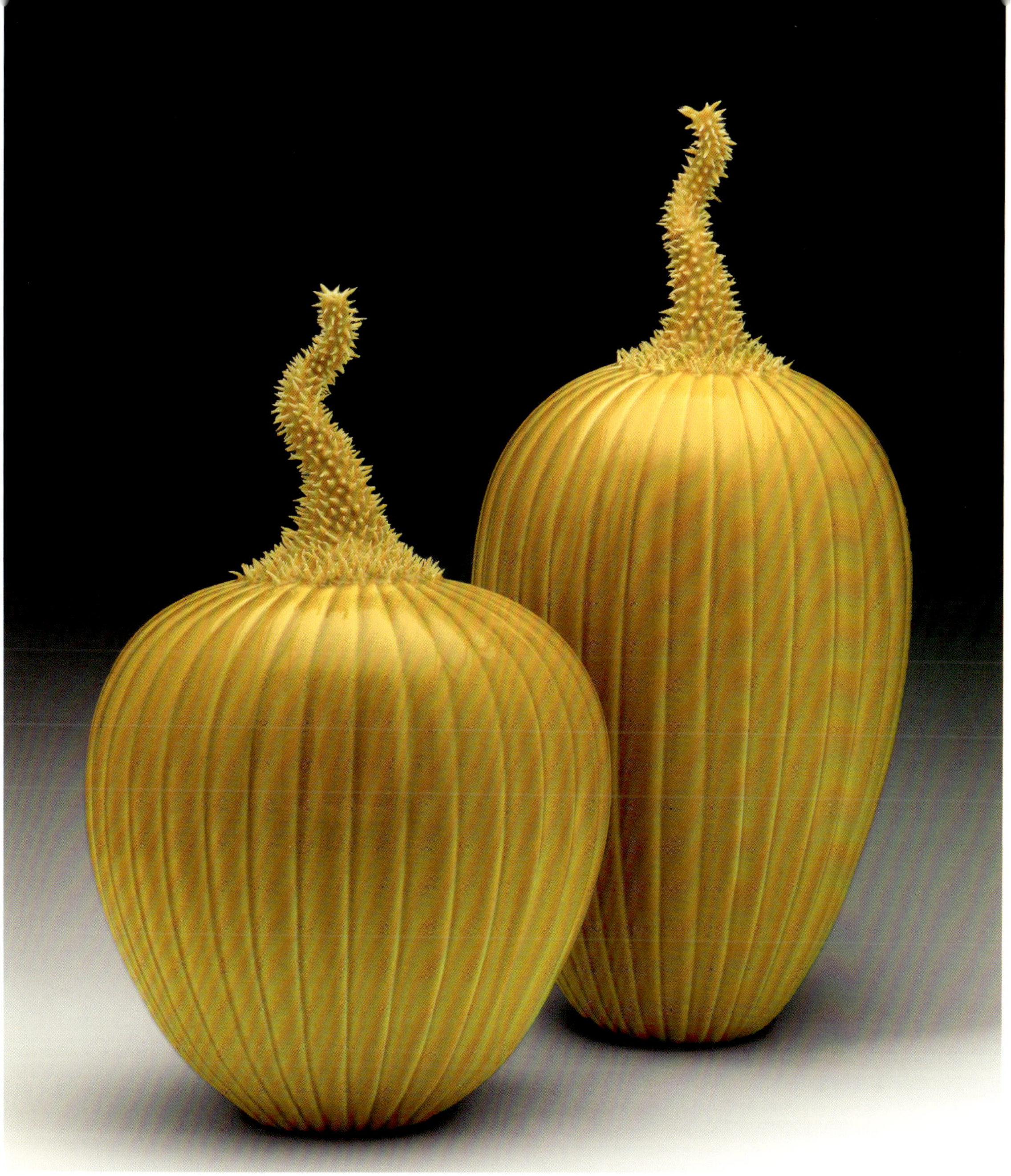

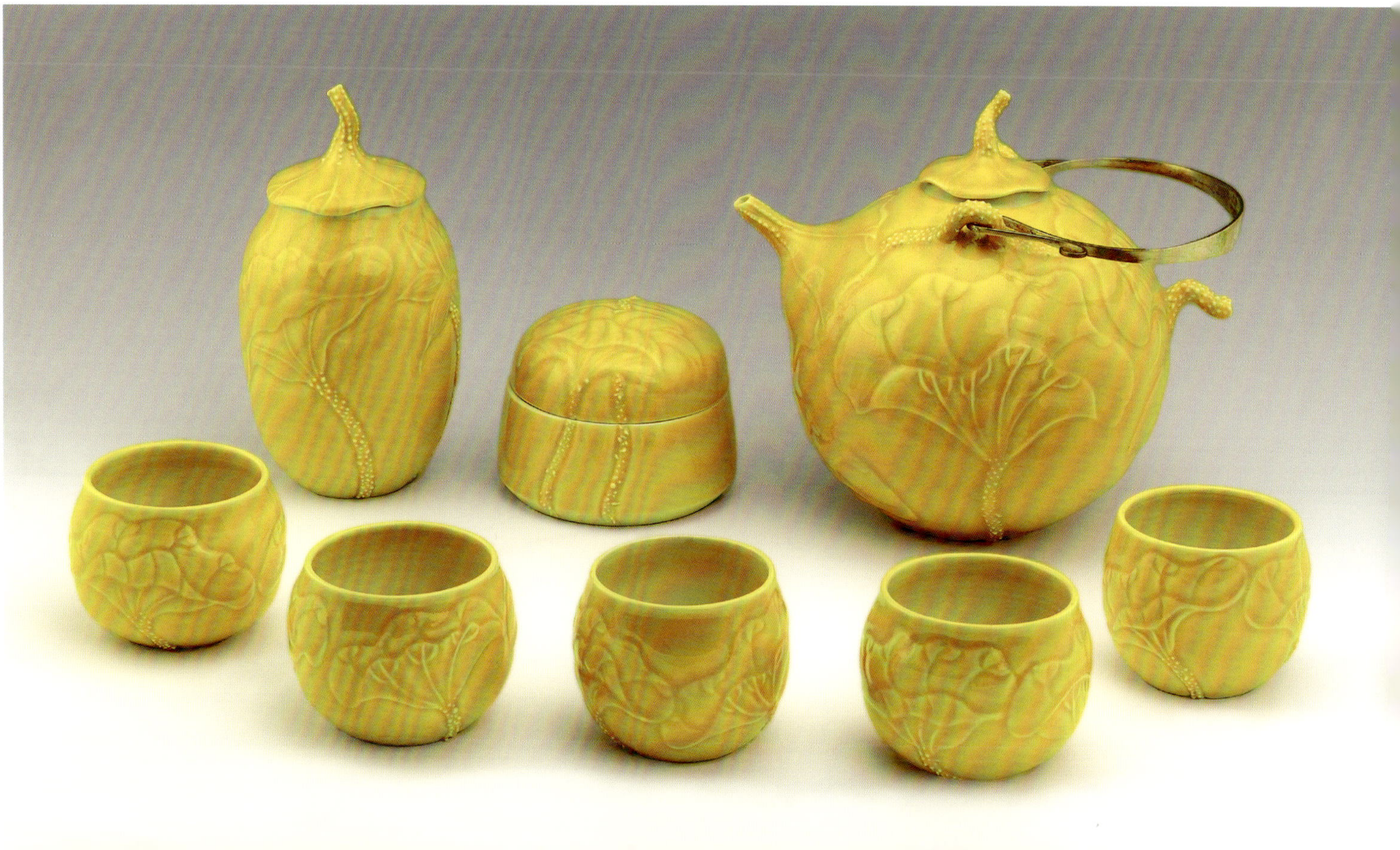

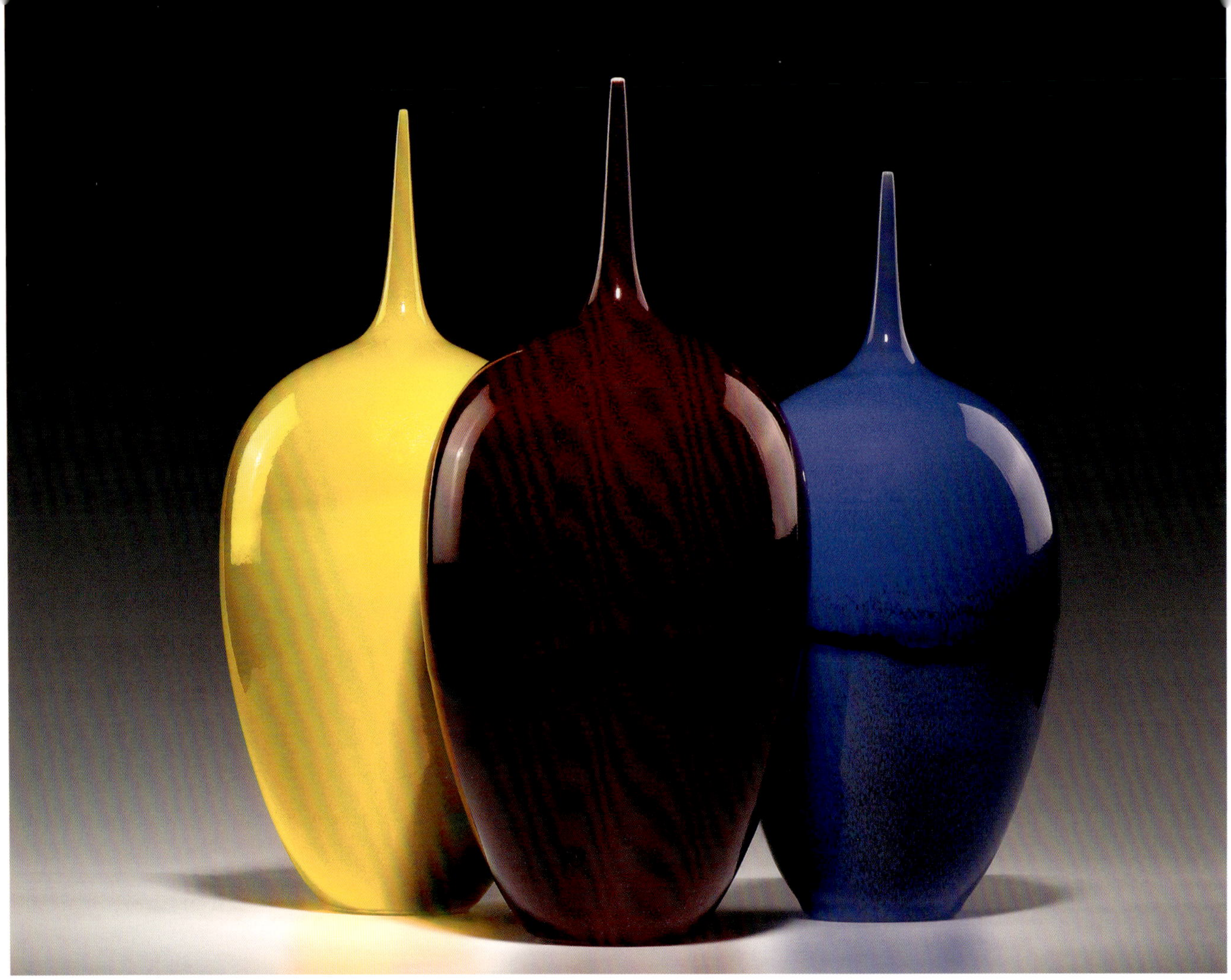

Fig. 27
***Teardrop*, 2001, porcelain and imperial yellow glaze. Collection of the artist**

***Teardrop*, 2001, porcelain and oxblood glaze. Collection of the artist**

***Teardrop*, 2004, porcelain and *chun* blue glaze. Collection of the artist**

Fig. 28
***Teardrop*, 2005, porcelain and peach bloom glaze. Collection of the artist**

the Southern Song (1127–1279) court after it was forced to relocate from Henan Province to modern-day Hangzhou, cutting off access to the previous official porcelain, *Ru* ware, the opaque blue color of which served as inspiration.[17] The fine crackle that distinguishes *guan* glaze is achieved through use of a higher percentage silica glaze that is deliberately underfired and cools faster than the vessel body, leading the glaze to fracture. It is then stained—with india ink in Lee's case (both ink and charcoal were used historically)—and can be refired several times to create overlapping layers of crackle.

Lee developed the teardrop shape in the late 1990s as a means of contemporizing the decorative vessel with a distinctly nonfunctional form that would serve as an uncomplicated backdrop to his glazes (fig. 30). His success is demonstrated by two fine examples, the sleek walls of which paradoxically mirror the gaze and invite it deep into the murky depths of a *temmoku* glaze. *Temmoku* (or *tenmoku*) is the Japanese term for the Chinese *tianmu,* the Southern Song dynasty blackwares from the province of Fujian that were introduced to Japan in the twelfth century by way of the Tianmu monastery near Hangzhou.[18] The family of iron-rich blacks and browns is partially responsible for the aesthetic development of formal teawares in Japan, one of the cultural touchstones for American studio ceramics. Yet Lee's examples do not display the earthy character often favored by his contemporaries; Lee has focused instead on the challenge of capturing consistency in color and texture across the glaze's surface. The reflective quality of the smaller teardrop is interrupted by a small patch of "hare's fur," which does more to highlight the uniformity of the remaining glaze than to mar it.[19]

The sumptuous olive green glaze known as tea dust is related to *temmoku* but presents a livelier side to the austere blacks Lee favors (fig. 31). Drastic reduction during firing allows crystallization to occur, which, along with increased levels of cobalt, lends the glaze its brilliant appearance and color. His fidelity to the original in tone and quality is evident in a Jingdezhen tripod bowl from the middle Qing dynasty; its original hardwood stand hints at a root to the design of porcelain stands for many of Lee's more opulent vessels (fig. 32).

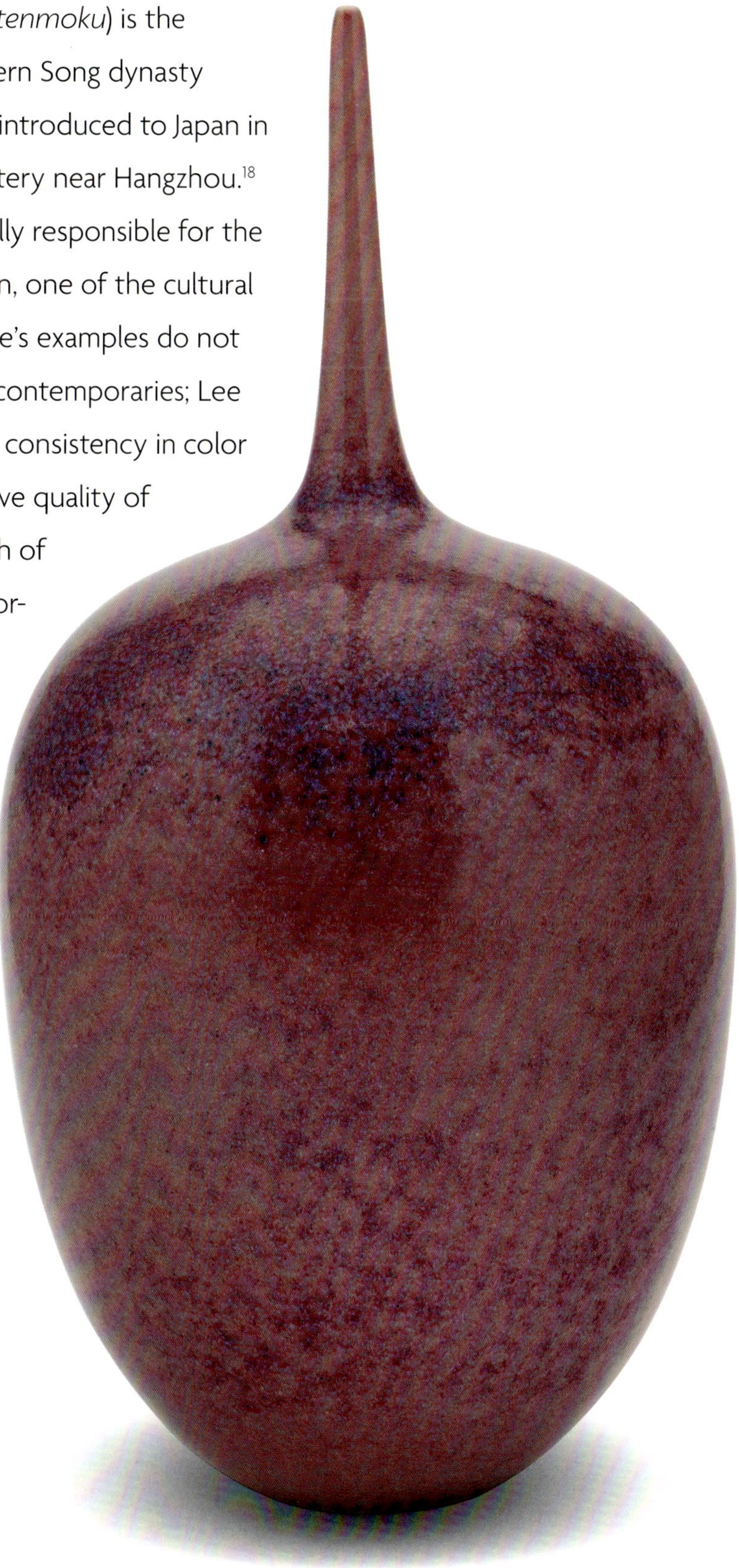

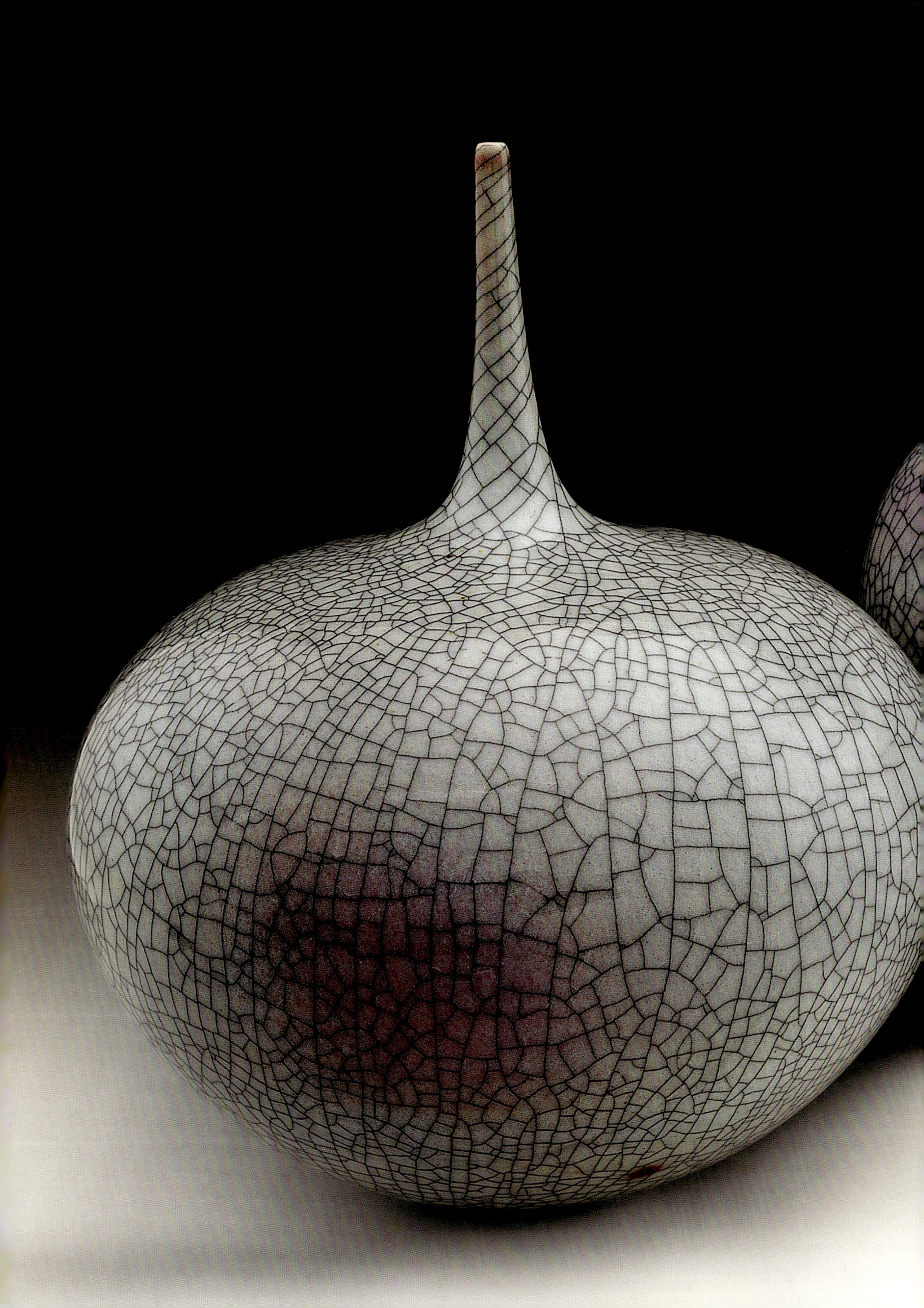

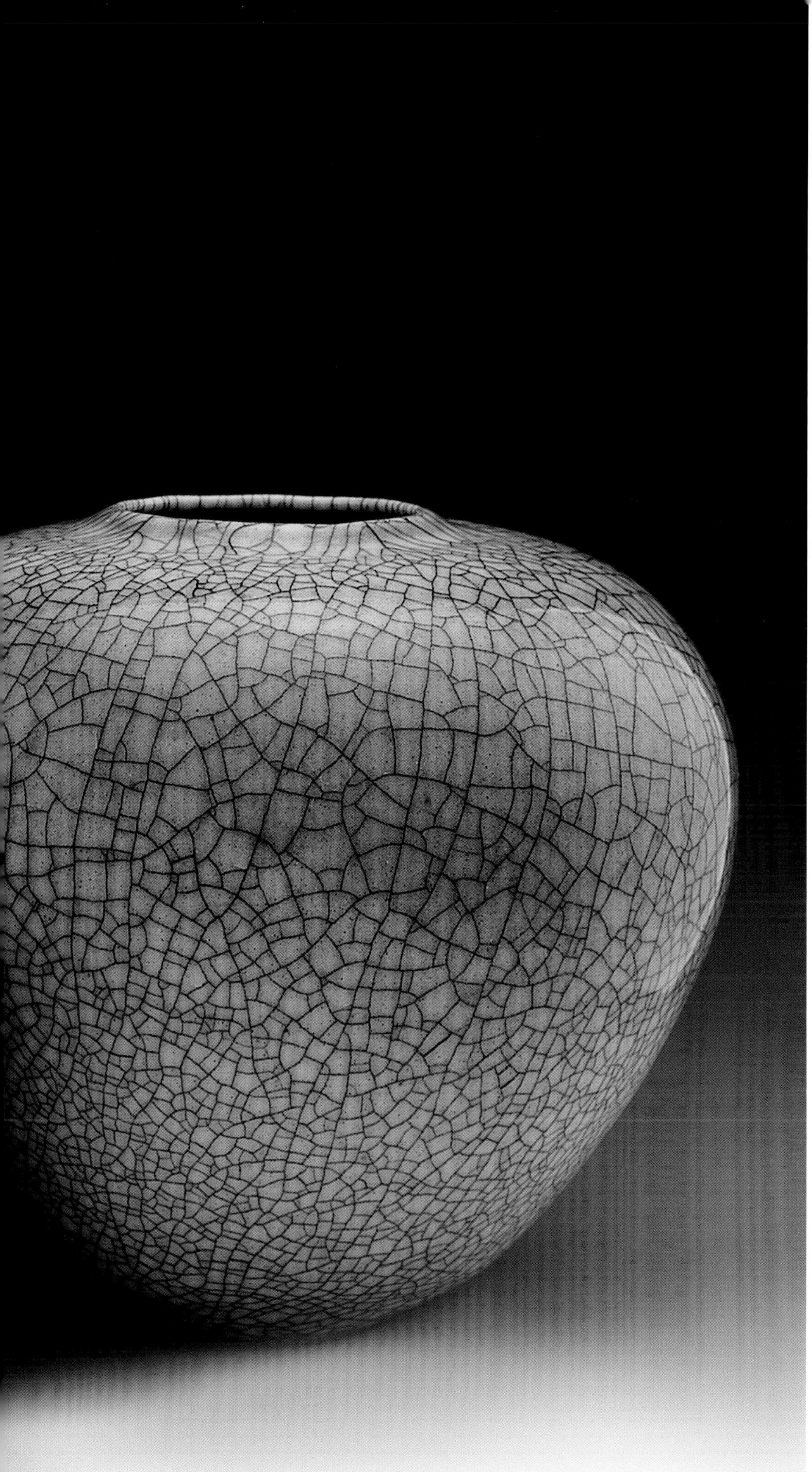

Fig. 29
Teardrop, 2000, porcelain, *guan* glaze, and india ink. Collection of Irwin and Marilyn Scher

Guan-ware Vase, 1994, porcelain, *guan* glaze, and india ink. Smithsonian American Art Museum, Gift of Carol and Bill Wright in memory of Dr. Edward L. Katz, 2010.36.5

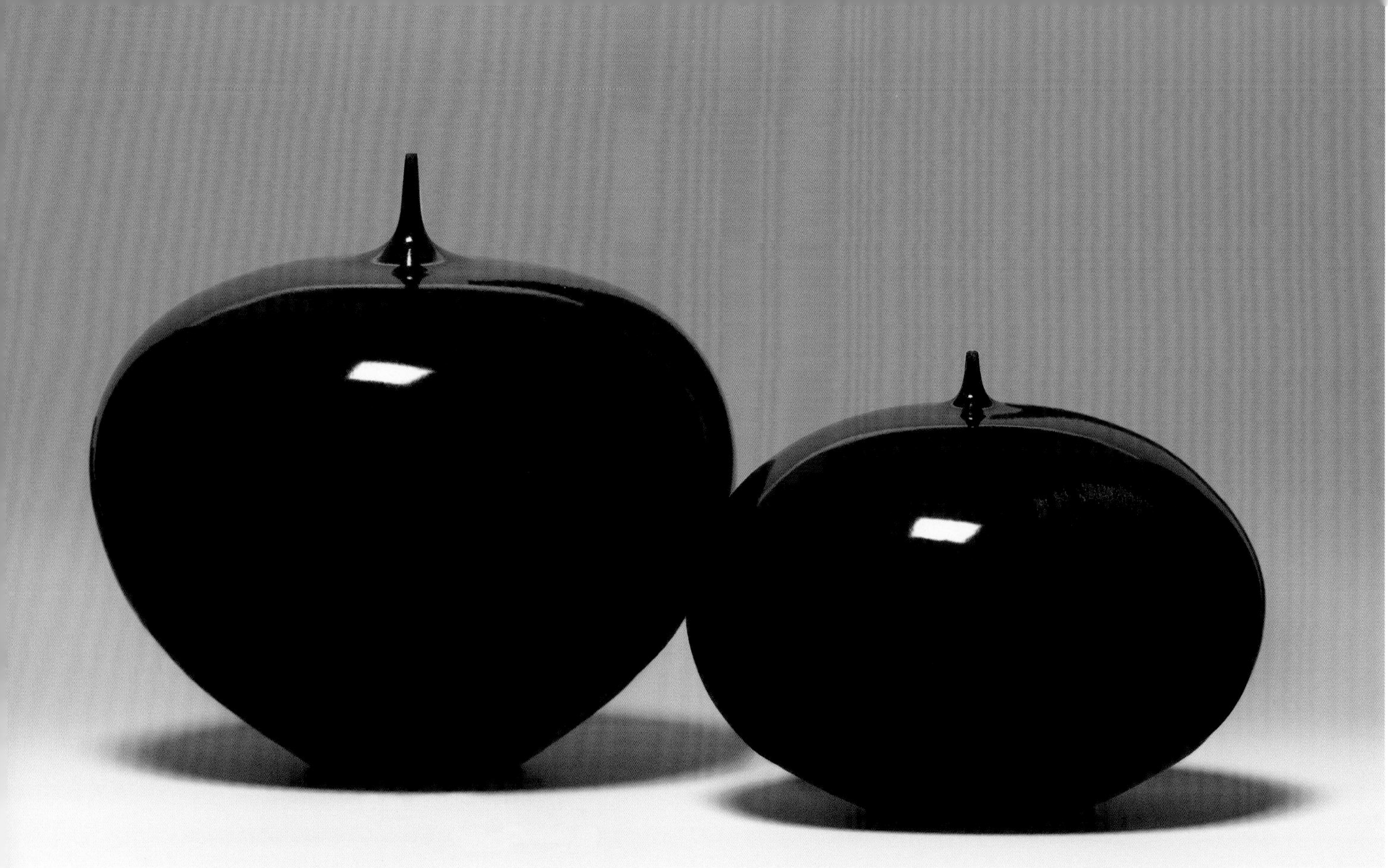

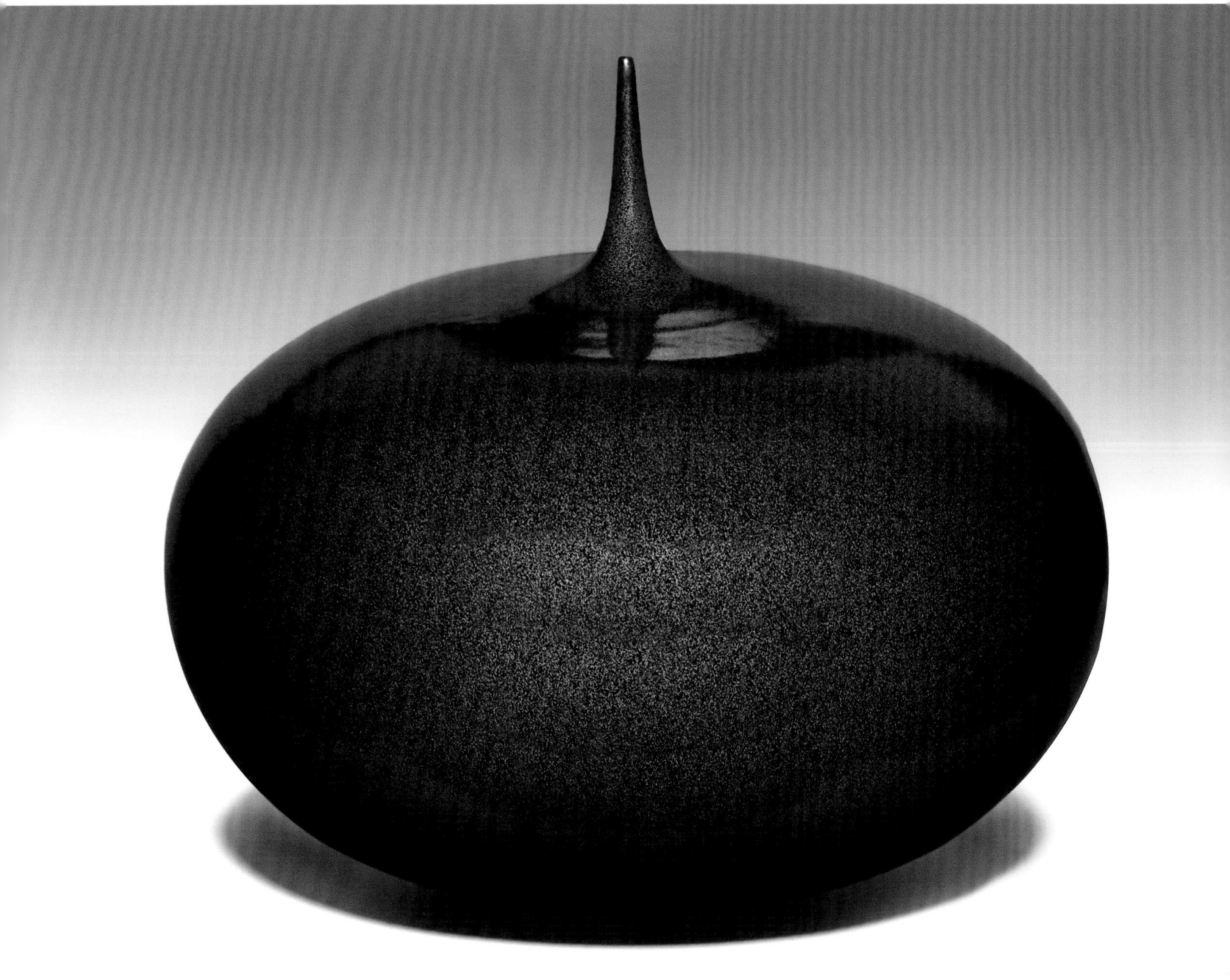

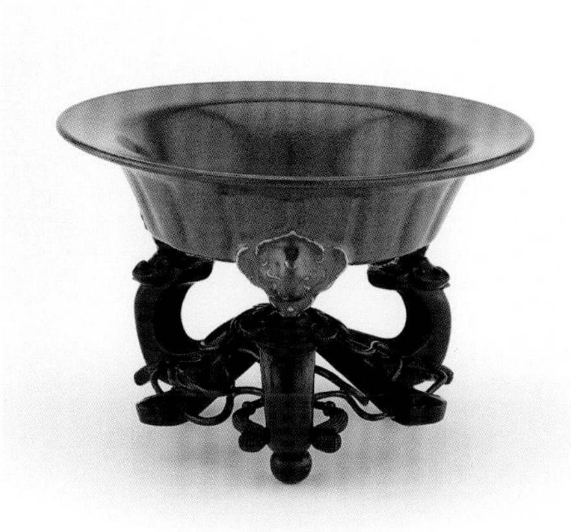

Two dramatic urns exhibit Lee's continued technical superiority in this temperamental medium, as well as his comfort in breaking away from the rigid historical inquiry that has dominated his development of glazes for decades (figs. 33, 34). His lava glaze (so called for its visual effect) is achieved through use of silicon carbide, which forms gas during firing and bubbles to the surface, causing it to crater; it is without direct precedent in Chinese ceramics (except perhaps in kiln accidents). The glaze's closest aesthetic neighbor in Asia is the rippled rather than cratered brown "snakeskin" glaze popular on Satsuma ware in nineteenth-century Japan.[20] Lava glazes were commonly employed in twentieth-century European ceramics and found continued influence in this country through their use by such studio potters as Otto and Getrud Natzler. Lee's proclivity for sculptural work is underscored by the fragility of some fired examples of lava, the foamlike surface of which is easily crushed by the untrained hand. "I'm a sadist," says Lee, "I like a challenge." At more than two feet high, these particular urns are a testament to this statement and his control of the material. The taller and thinner the unfired porcelain vessel, the more likely it is to collapse under its own weight as it rests, often for weeks, between the wheel and the kiln. Lee counts the firing and survival of works at this scale as among his most satisfying

Fig. 30
***Teardrop*, 2000, porcelain and *temmoku* glaze. Collection of the artist**

***Teardrop*, 2001, porcelain and *temmoku* glaze. Collection of the artist**

Fig. 31
***Teardrop*, 2004, porcelain and tea dust glaze. Collection of the artist**

Fig. 32
Unidentified artist, *Tripod Bowl with Wooden Stand,* 1736–95, porcelain, tea dust glaze, hardwood stand, 2 5/8 × 8 × 8 in. Freer Gallery of Art, Smithsonian Institution, Washington, DC, Purchase—Friends of Asian Art, F1994.3a-b

Fig. 33
Lychee Nut Urn, 2010, porcelain and lava glaze. Collection of the artist

Fig. 34
Lychee Nut Urn, 2010, porcelain and lava glaze. Collection of the artist

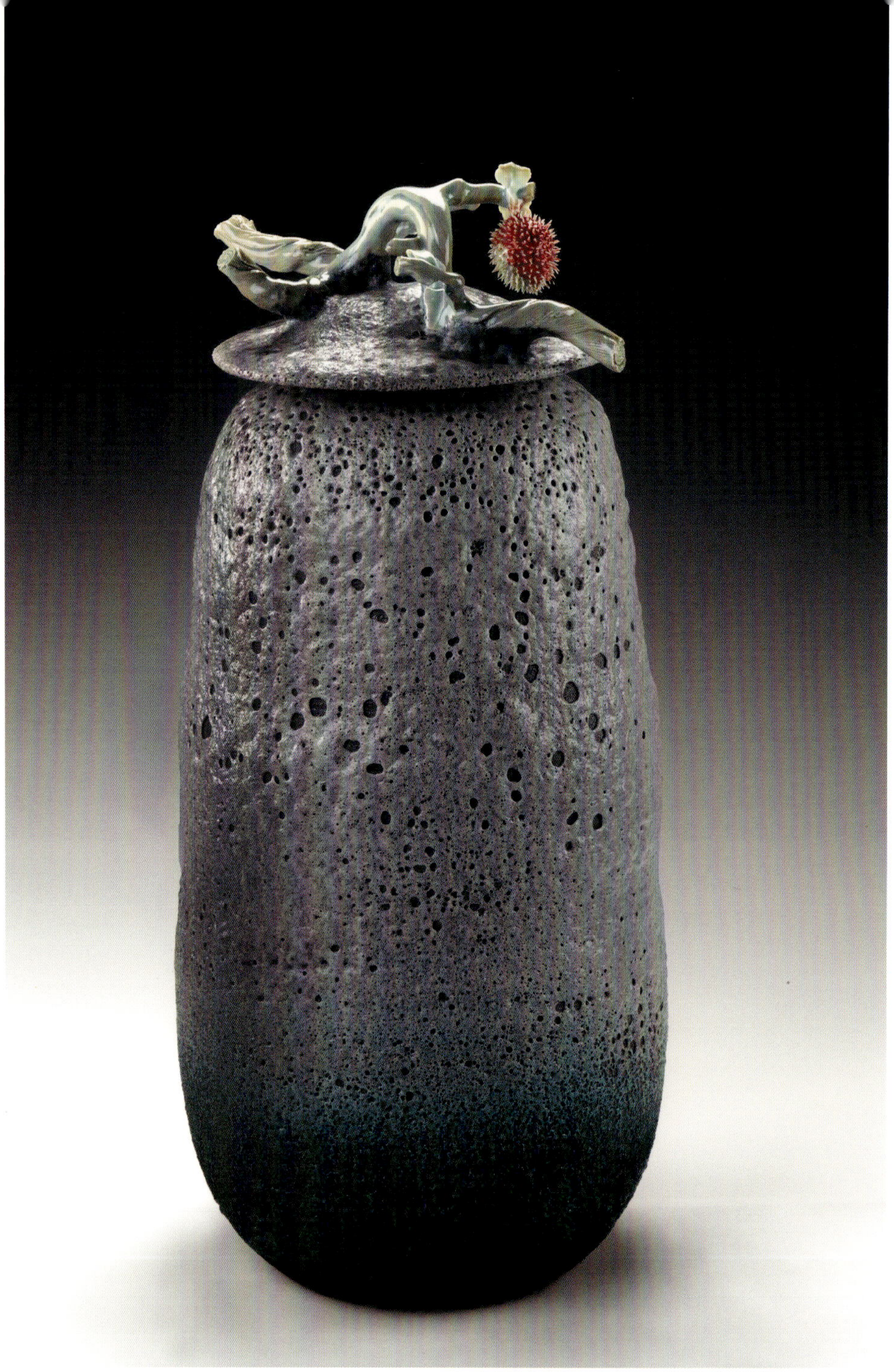

recent technical achievements. The lychee nuts atop their lids are a token of remembrance for the prickly fruit that grew in the backyard of his boyhood home in Kaohsiung. Modestly, they draw his work full circle to a time when Cliff Lee was still a diplomat's son, standing in front of an old porcelain vase.

NICHOLAS R. BELL

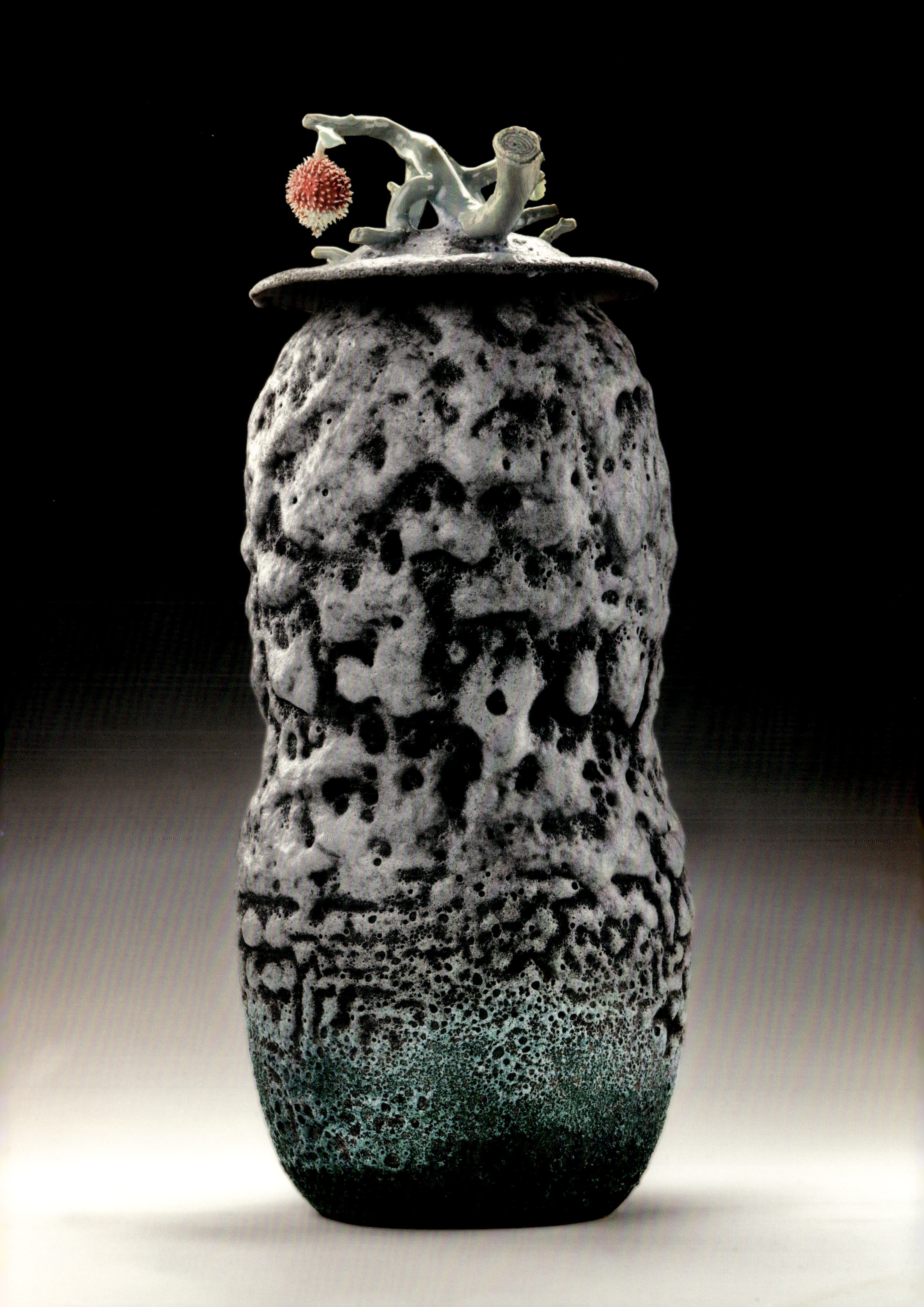

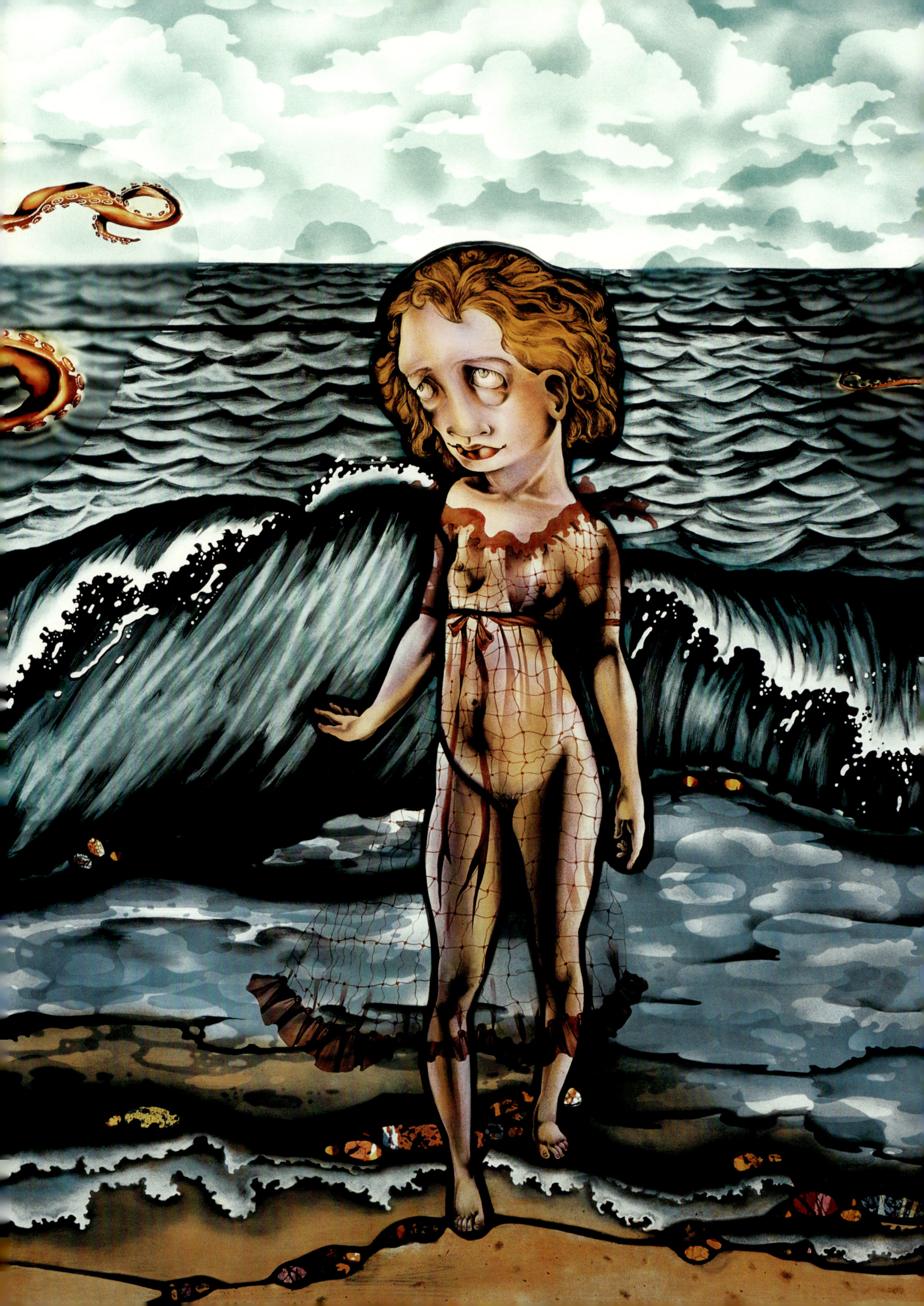

judith schaechter

Judith Schaechter has a complex relationship with beauty. In a talk she recently gave at the Observatory Room in Brooklyn, New York, the stained glass artist warned against intellectualizing the subject: "I am not interested in *ideas* of beauty. I don't find it thought provoking. On the contrary, I find beauty to be thought annihilating."[21] Schaechter is enamored, if not obsessed, with what she describes as the emotional, sensual experience of beauty.

This assessment would be not entirely obvious from a cursory glance at her work—stained glass windows depicting pale, ghostly figures often in the throes of death surrounded by skulls, beckoning angels, and other symbols of the afterlife (fig. 35). But don't doubt it: Schaechter is really into beauty. She has thought about it more than

***Dream of the Fisherman's Wife* (detail), 2004 (see p. 100)**

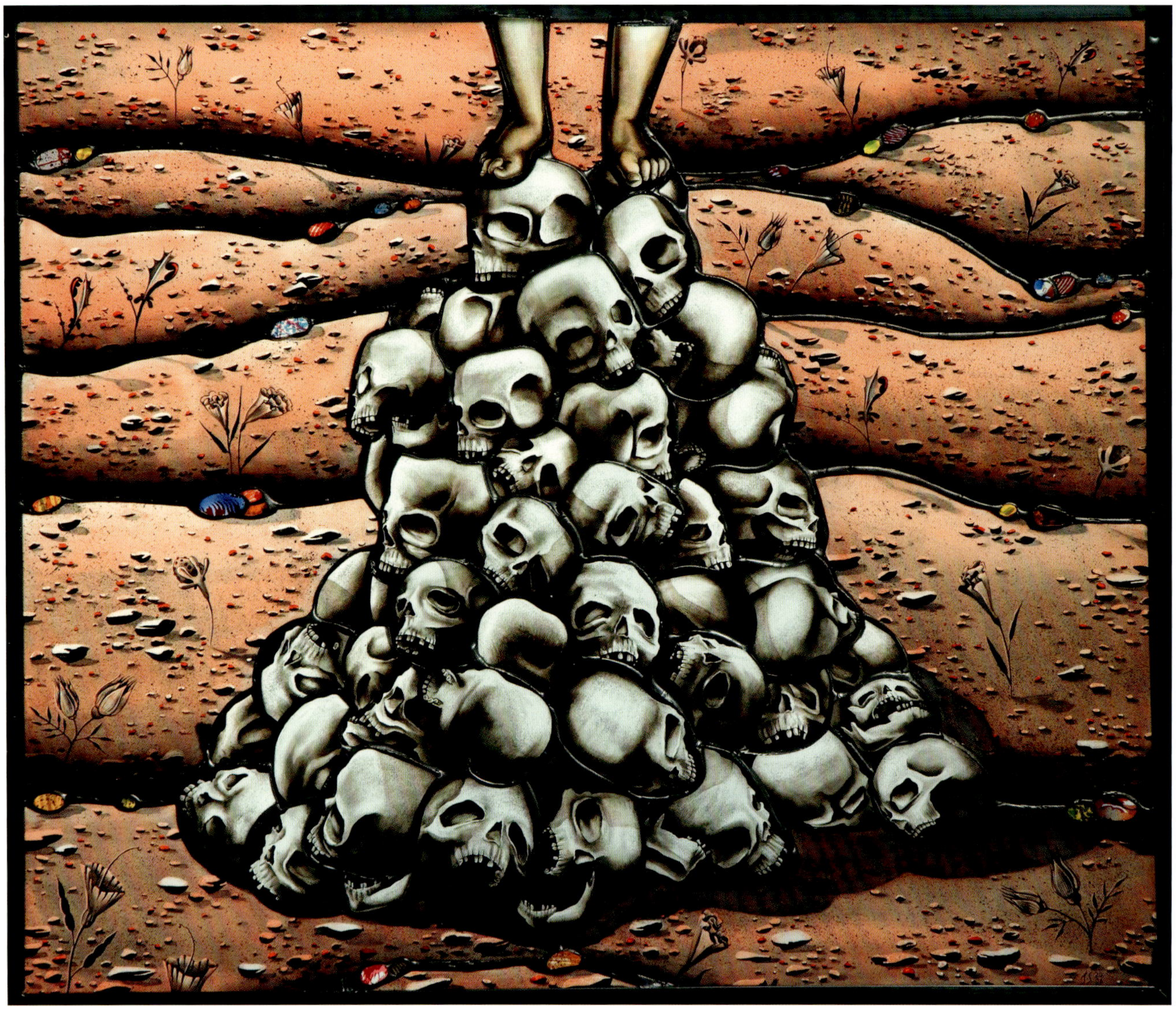

Fig. 35
***Monument*, 2006, glass.**
Collection of Ryan and Joanna Scott

most and can talk about it in her distinctive, cutting voice for hours, keeping an audience enthralled with twinges of self-deprecating humor and poignant insight. "Beauty," the longtime Philadelphia resident is quick to point out, "has very little to do with 'pretty'." She'll also remind you that notions of ugliness are important too. True beauty, Schaechter will tell you, is about the push and pull between the two. "Beauty's vastness," she says, "is the only thing that can contain both."

Schaechter seems to have realized this dichotomy from an early age. She is fond of recounting her childhood in Newton, Massachusetts, and her trips to the Museum of Fine Arts in Boston—accompanied by her mother, a pianist, and her father, a microbiologist at Tufts University—where she was continually drawn to the "scary paintings"[22] (fig. 36); those visits later influenced her work, including *Judith and the Head of Holofernes,* 2002 (fig. 37). But she also recalls her discomfort in her own skin and always being curious about the "pretty" people she saw around her every day. And it was those two competing interests that perhaps led her to the Judith Schaechter we know today—the artist who has painstakingly and meticulously not only mastered what many consider a dying craft but also managed to invigorate it with new life and purpose, to take the ancient art of stained glass making and inject it with contemporary forms and content while never straying from the traditions for which she has the utmost respect.

After high school, Schaechter found herself in Providence, studying painting at the Rhode Island School of Design (RISD). Although painting was her chosen medium—her grandmother, who learned to paint in her seventies, encouraged Schaechter from a young age—it also intimidated her. A blank canvas always made the artist nervous, and when she took a class in stained glass during her first years of school, she was sold. Schaechter graduated from RISD in 1983, moved to Philadelphia, and never looked back. Stained glass has accompanied her each step of the way, evolving with her every move and helping the artist to define herself in ways painting might never have touched.

Stained glass is a notoriously difficult medium, demanding seemingly unending hours of manual labor. In the end, the tedium involved in making a piece is a large part of what drew Schaechter to the art form. A 2009

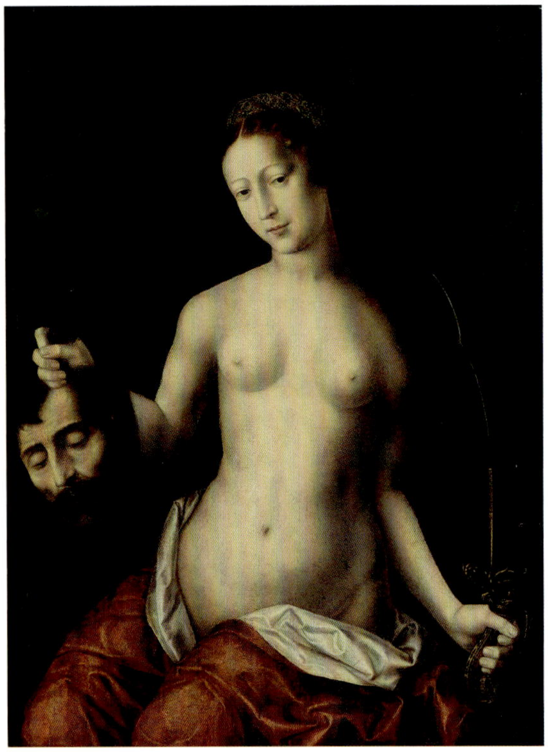

article in *American Craft* by Robert Sullivan perfectly captures Schaechter's love of the process. Sullivan quoted the artist: "'With glass you have to do this.' She points to her tools, to the painstakingly etched glass. 'You have to put the contact paper on. You have to grind this. You have to sandblast there. And there's all this *stuff* that has to be done to it before *anything* has happened. By the time you are done you love it like a baby because you have gestated it'"[23] (fig. 38).

Having been an adjunct professor at the Philadelphia School of the Arts for more than fifteen years, Schaechter has become adept at explaining her work in laymen's terms and has honed a remarkable patience for newcomers who show interest. A typical window consists of hundreds of individual pieces of flash glass in hundreds of colors. The pieces are sandblasted, stitched together using copper foil and solder, then baked in a high-temperature kiln; a finished work might measure around thirty by forty inches. Schaechter says she could probably finish a window in two to three weeks if she wasn't so picky, putting everything together only to pull it all apart and start over. Schaechter's studio is piled high with boxes containing her various miscues labeled lovingly with names like "crap," "rejects," and "bulk failure."

Fig. 36
Jan Massys, Netherlandish (1509–1575), *Judith with the Head of Holofernes*, 1543, oil on panel, 40 ¼ × 29 ¾ in. Museum of Fine Arts, Boston, Abbott Lawrence Fund and Picture Fund, 12.1048

Fig. 37
***Judith and the Head of Holofernes*, 2002, glass. Collection of Ali K. Fard and Edward Simpson**

Explaining the work that goes into producing these mishaps—not to mention her masterpieces—Schaechter says, using one recent piece as an

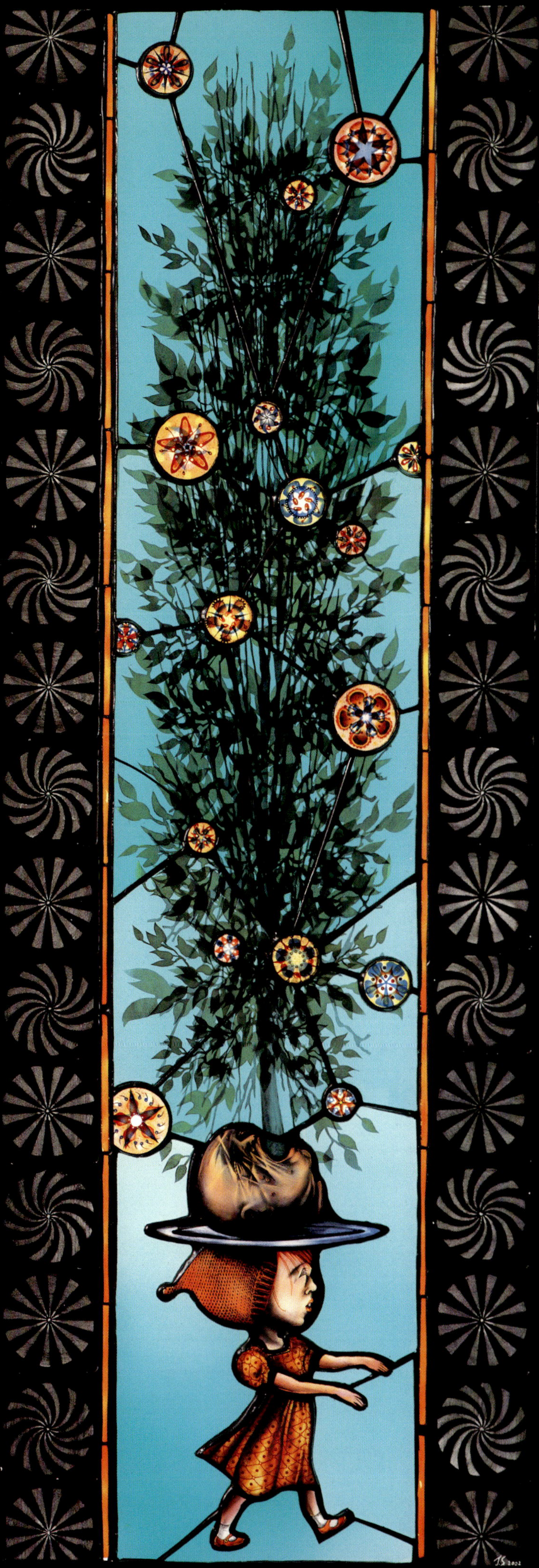

Fig. 38
***Self-Portrait of Someone Else*, 2009, glass. Private collection**

example, "You place red glass on clear glass. The red-on-clear layer is sand-blasted and then engraved with a flexible shaft drill and a diamond file." Standard technique, right? "Oh, hell no!" Schaechter is quick to exclaim. "No, no, no! Most stained glass artists sandblast a little but not very much. Flash glass is really expensive; they don't like to use it." And her novel use of the diamond file? "I think I invented the whole diamond file thing."[24]

"Diamond files . . . are for lamp workers to smooth out the edges of their beads," she continues. "But I use them to smooth out tones in my pieces. I rough out the glass with the sandblaster. I go between rough and delicate with the flexible shaft engraver, and then I go into it with the diamond file to make these really smooth gradations. Then I paint the glass with vitreous paint. I then fire it on at 1,213 degrees in a kiln." That process is repeated for each individual section of the larger work. "The easiest way to think of my process," Schaechter says, "is like color separation. So many people think I'm painting on my colors. I am not. I'm removing color. Not adding it."[25]

Schaechter's work has been a stroke of genius and innovation since the early days of her career. Her methods—engraving, layering, sand-blasting—are unorthodox and rarely seen outside her Philadelphia studio. She consistently challenges conventions in the craft, bringing her rabble-rouser attitude to glass and kiln. This approach has cemented her place in the small, rarified world of stained glass makers as a master crafts-person and visionary artist.

Like all great works of art, Schaechter's pieces give the illusion of ease. They appear effortless in their execution, which, of course, is the

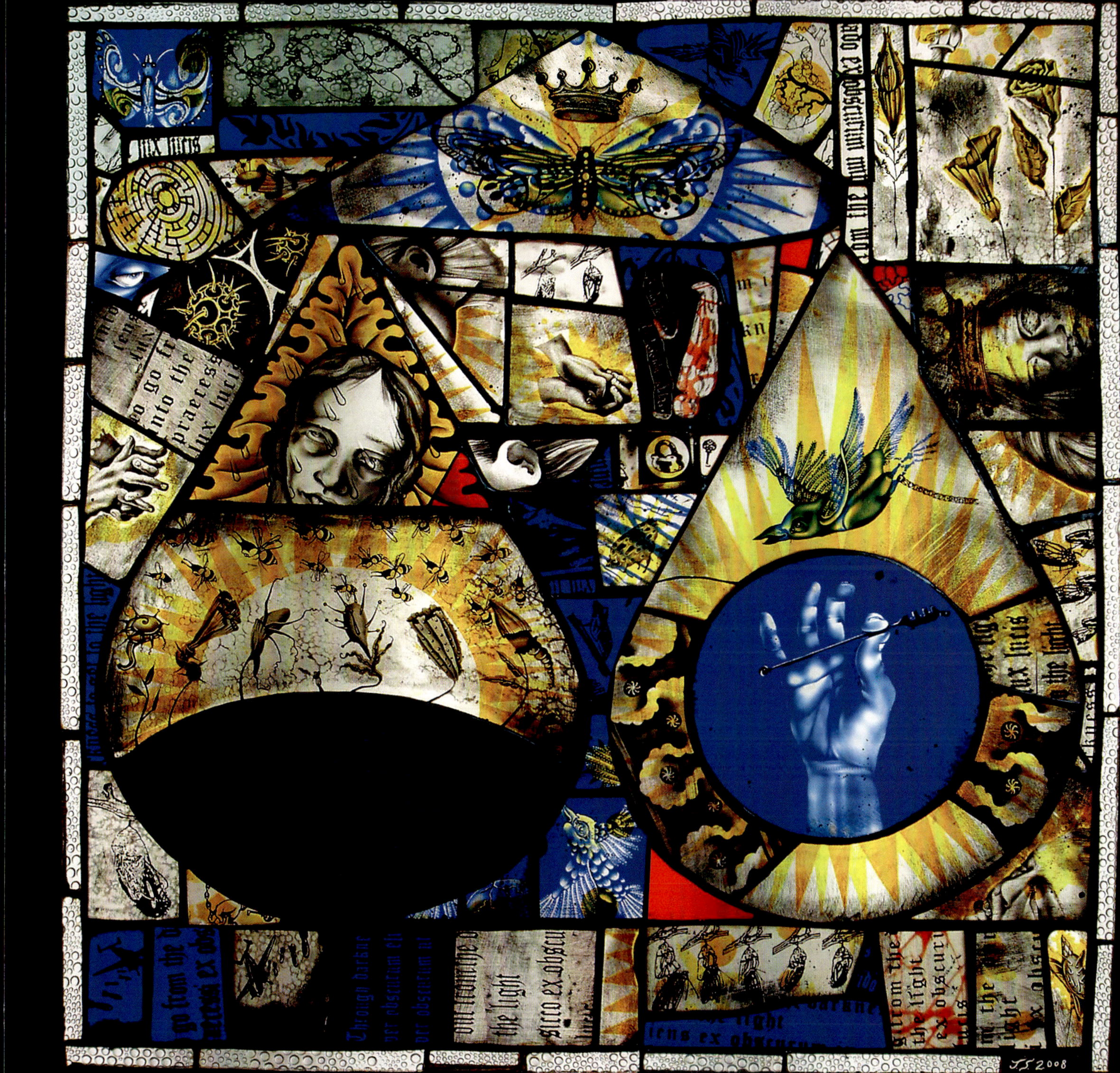
lux lucis
to go fr
into the
praecess
lux luci
J.S. 2008

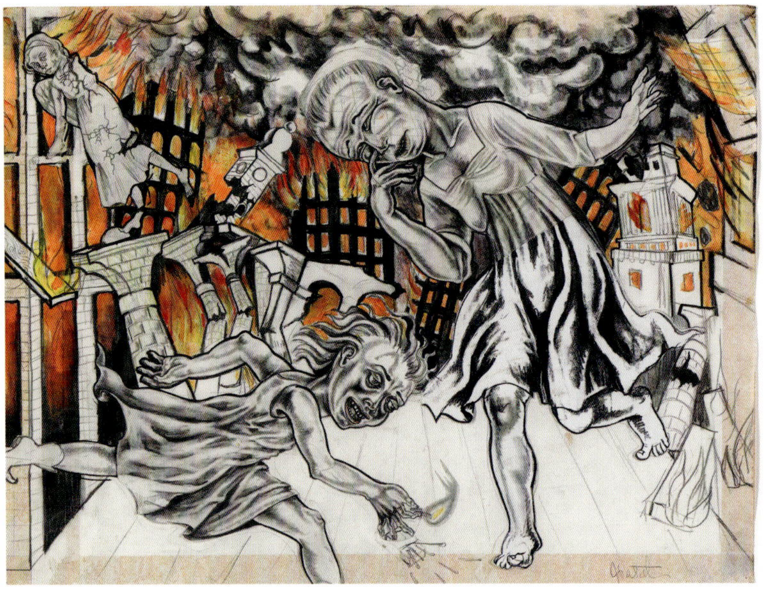

furthest thing from the truth. The physically heavy work hangs lightly in place, whether in museums, galleries, or living rooms. Pieces such as *A Little Torcher* (figs. 39, 40) sit quietly, not weighted down by their materiality yet commanding attention with their implied tales of mortality, morality, and historical tales of loss and regret.

Schaechter, not surprisingly, is taken with her own familial history. In particular, she has often focused her attention on the life of her great-great-great-uncle, John Fletcher Hamlin (fig. 41), a Civil War soldier who died at the age of twenty-one and whom she commemorates in *John Fletcher Hamlin Is No More* (fig. 42). This interest perhaps has also led to her curiosity in Victorian-era mourning rituals and traditions. On her Web site, Schaechter lists her inspirations in running order: "Cemeteries and cemetery art… old New England graveyards, the Gettysburg battlefield, of course, but also lots of other stuff related to death piques my interest—I am interested in death in general. I mean, aren't we all on some level? . . . Civil War letters are amazingly beautiful and a tonic to all that is cynical and ironic in our world today."[26] All of this plays into Schaechter's elaborate tales told in spectacular detail through masterful workmanship rendered in glass. Each of Schaechter's pieces is a lesson in the results

Fig. 39
Sketch for *A Little Torcher,* 1990, paper. Collection of Elmerina and Paul Parkman

Fig. 40
***A Little Torcher,* 1990, glass. Smithsonian American Art Museum, Gift of the James Renwick Alliance and museum purchase through the Smithsonian Institution Collections Acquisition Program, 1991.83**

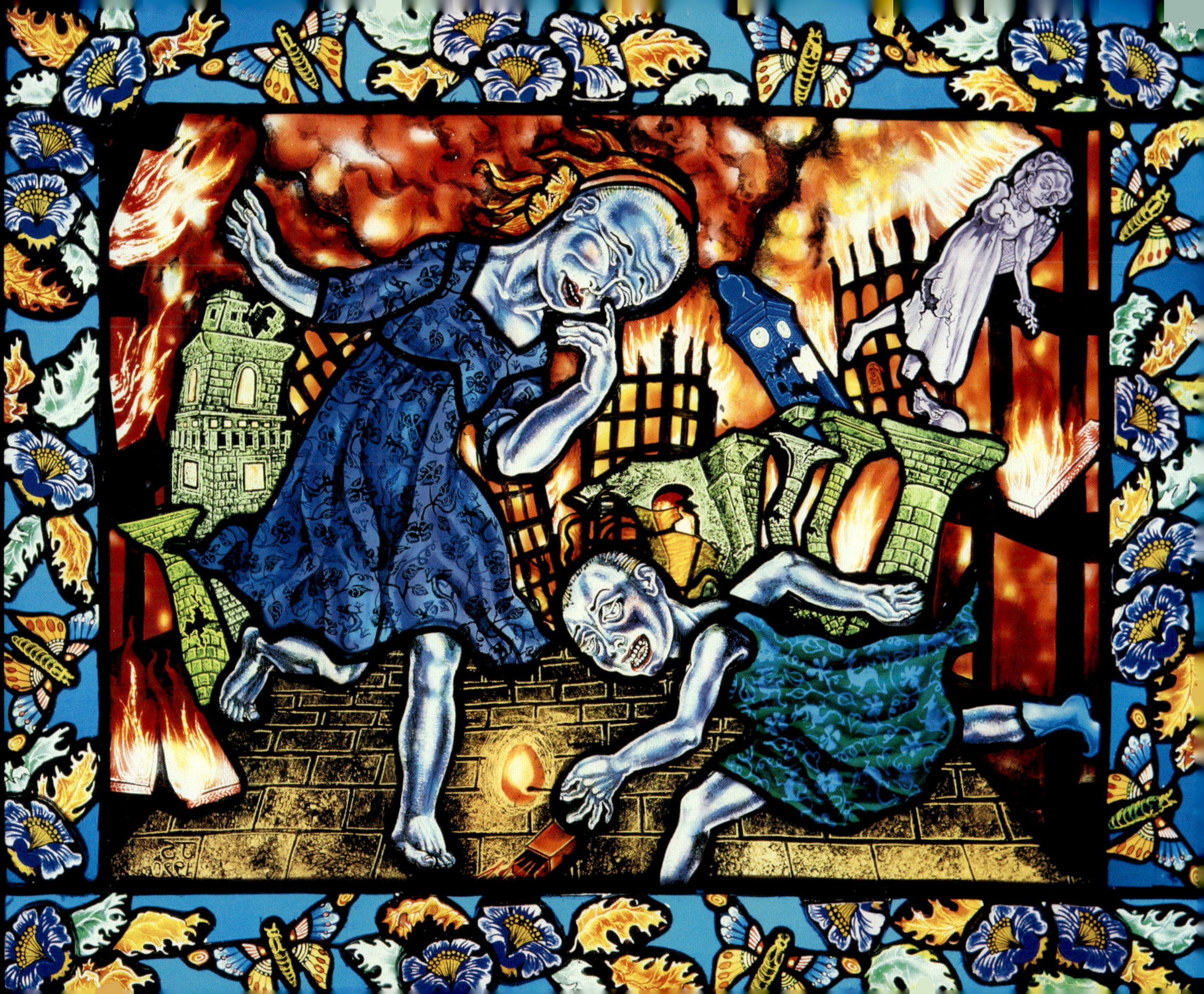

Fig. 41
Photographer unknown, *John Fletcher Hamlin*, 1863, paper. Collection of the artist

Fig. 42
***John Fletcher Hamlin Is No More*, 2003, glass. Collection of Dr. David Mittleman and Mr. Hugh Glatts**

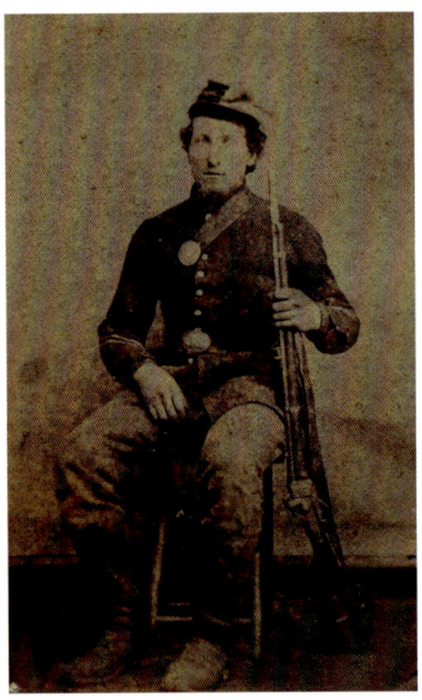

that intellectual fervor mixed with rare craftsmanship and old-fashioned hard work can produce (fig. 43).

Maybe it is all of this hard work that has led Schaechter to beauty, because in Schaechter's book, the word is not to be taken lightly. "Beautiful is a sacrosanct term reserved for the extra special peak aesthetic experience that appeals to our soul as well as to our senses," she explains. "Beauty is the transformative experience of being filled with desire and inspiration." Whereas *pretty* and *ugly* appeal on very base levels, beautiful is something much deeper, much more visceral. And to get to that deeper level one has to work—both as the artist and the viewer.

Beauty is awe inducing, but as Schaechter often points out and her work demonstrates, "there is a dark side. Beauty can be so powerful it can transform meaninglessness and atrocity into a union with the cosmic." And, Schaechter states, "The impact of beauty is nothing short of fierce. [The Harvard psychologist] Nancy Etcoff points out that many of the words we use to qualify beauty are violent: bombshell, knockout, drop-dead gorgeous. Rapturous…This is how badly we want it; this is what we are willing to risk getting it. Beauty provokes a gut 'WOW!' response, which is why I call it 'thought annihilating'—it doesn't really appeal to the intellect." A powerful sentiment to be sure, but Schaechter takes it a step further, saying "Because this experience is so glorious, so fleeting, mysterious, erotic, traumatic even, it is always calling attention to its own inevitable loss. Therefore, beauty embodies a healthy measure of anxiety and fear. It takes courage to take the risks of engaging beauty."

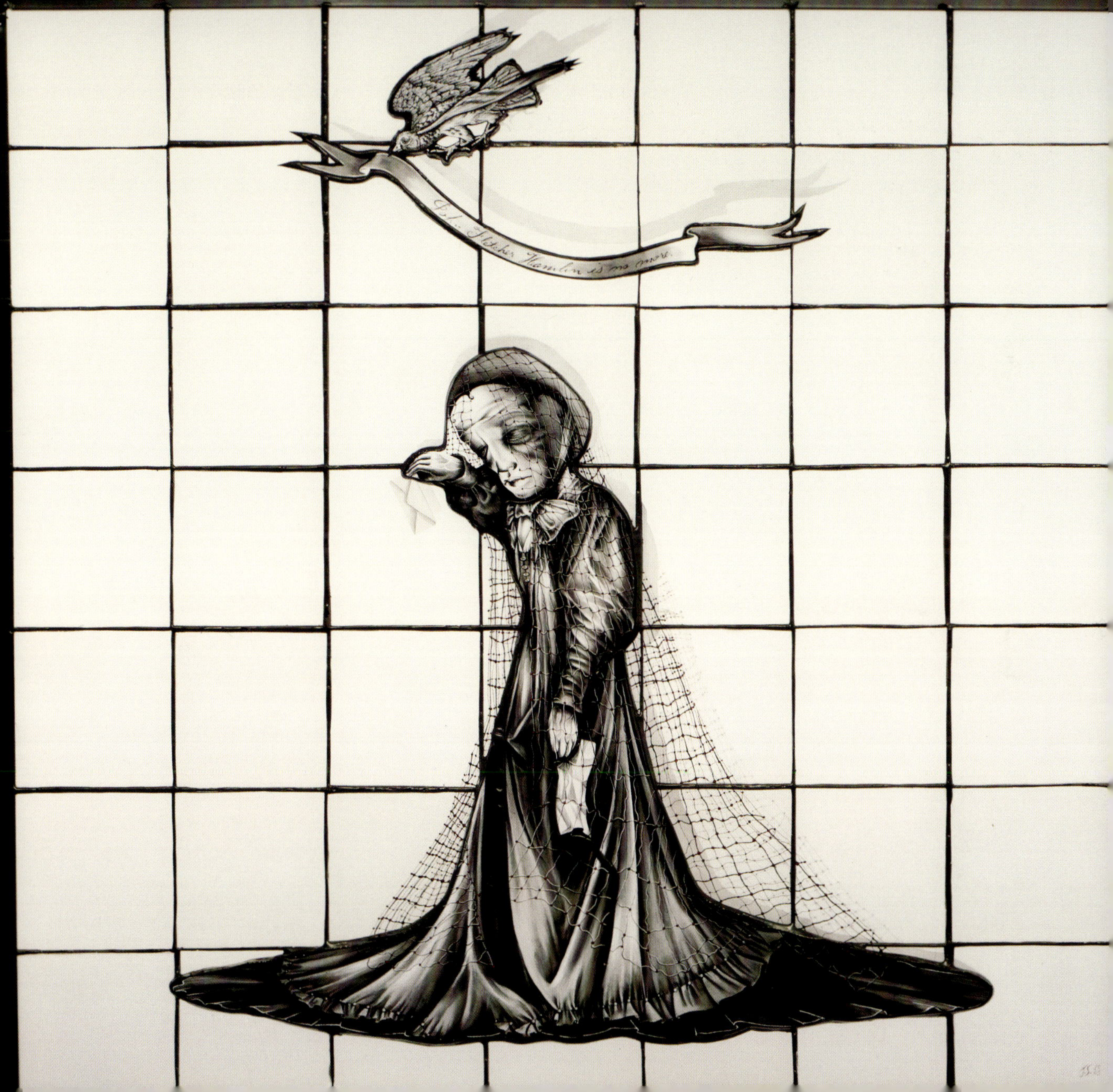
Fletcher Hamlin is no more.

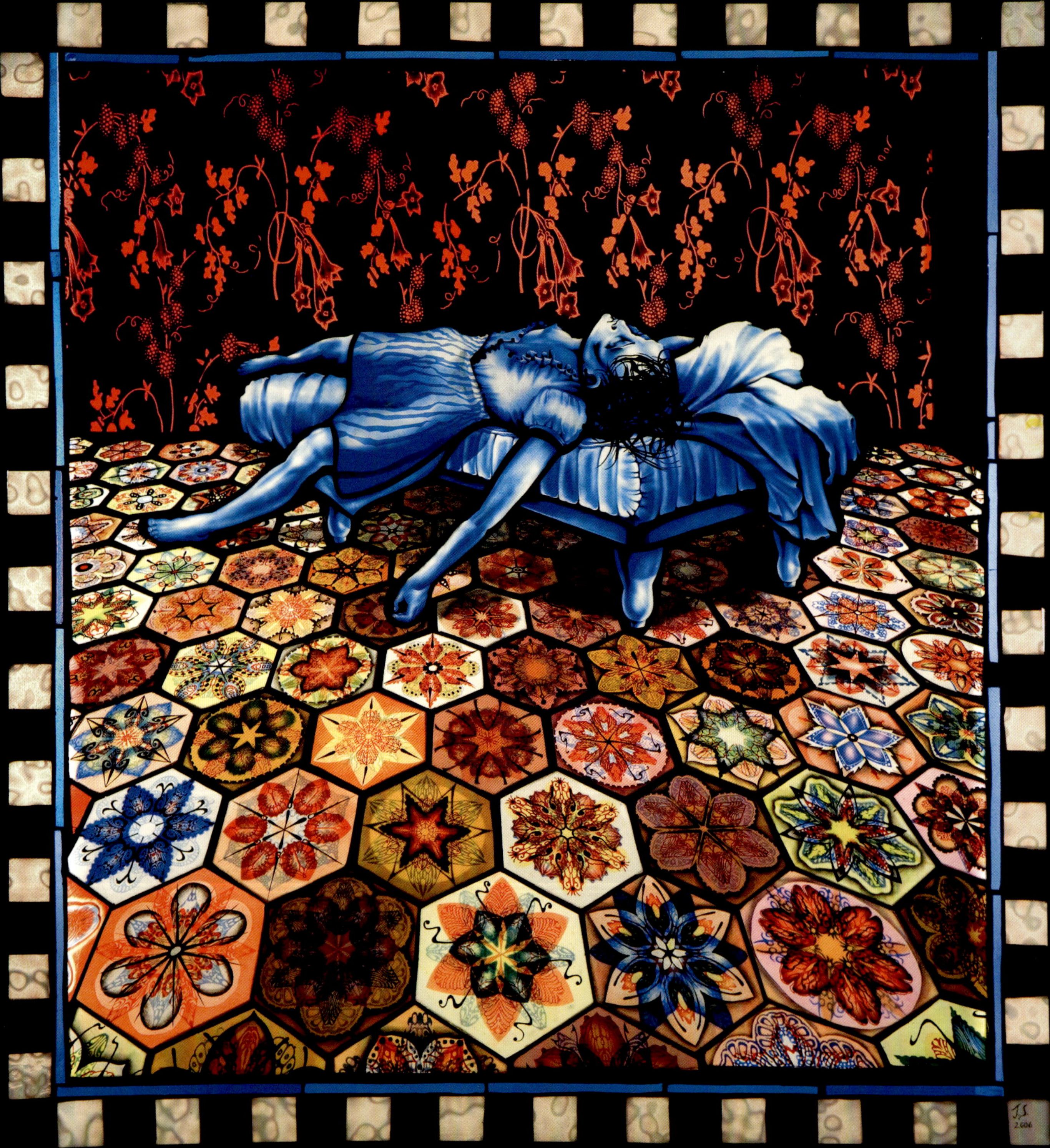
J.S.
2006

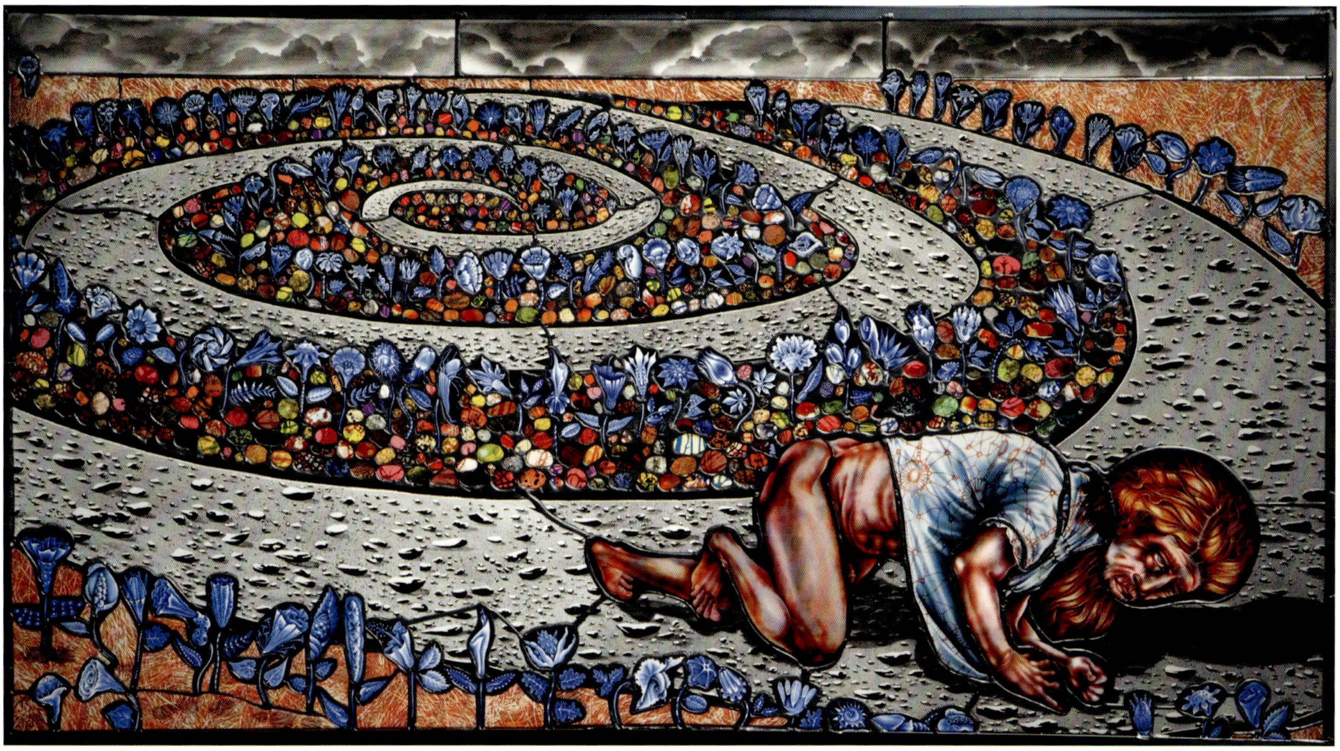

Much of Schaechter's work presents these risks and challenges viewers to engage on a level that is often uncomfortable. Newer pieces such as *The Sin Eater* and *An Invocation* (figs. 44, 45) work in much the same way that stained glass in centuries-old European chapels do: you are awed by their presence, taken in by their color and vivid imagery, and eventually left with an impression of a story that is much deeper than the thin layers of glass used to create the work. The experience often leaves you on edge. Yes, the work presents sensual pop and pulses with energy, but it also reveals a very real, ugly side of life that a viewer cannot ignore. The combination of the two contrasting elements (pretty

Fig. 43
***The Floor,* 2006, glass. Collection of Claire Oliver and Ian Rubinstein**

Fig. 44
***The Sin Eater,* 2010, glass. Courtesy of the artist and Claire Oliver Gallery, New York**

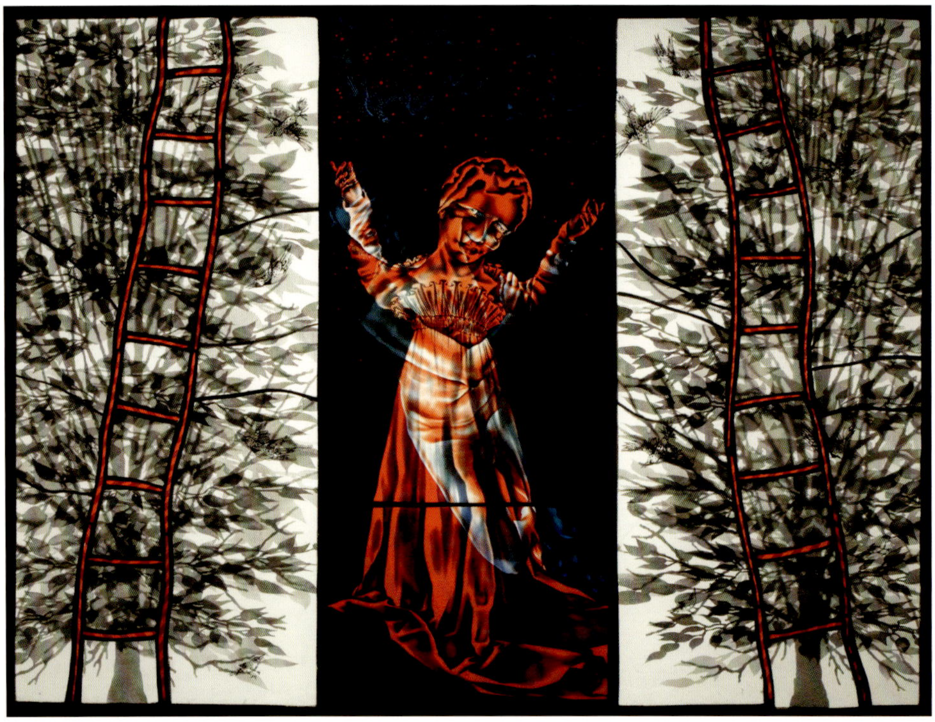

Fig. 45
***An Invocation*, 2009, glass. Courtesy of the artist and Claire Oliver Gallery, New York**

Fig. 46
***My One Desire*, 2007, glass. Collection of Todd Alios VonBastiaans**

and ugly) equates to a whole that is neither comforting nor entirely discomforting. Schaechter's work leaves you in a new place, one you may never have thought of venturing to on your own.

And that is precisely what Schaechter is striving for: the elusive idea of beauty that is deep and challenging. Beauty that is imparted on the world not necessarily to make us feel this way or that, but to make us feel. To wake us up and make us consider the beauty that is hidden all around us. The beauty that lies in the simplest of forms. As Schaechter says, "There is something about beauty that is familiar, yet unique. Obvious, yet mysterious. Easy, yet difficult. Comfortable, yet disturbing. Lovely, yet hateful. And in every case, a lot in between."

It is those in-betweens that Schaechter is intent on mining, searching the cracks and crevices for the unique and often the forgotten, and giving those ideas and forms a voice, a proper place in the world. And in doing so, Schaechter, whether she cares to admit it or not, sometimes hits upon beauty (figs. 46, 47). Often it is the simple act of finding one's place in the world that suddenly ups one's attractiveness by

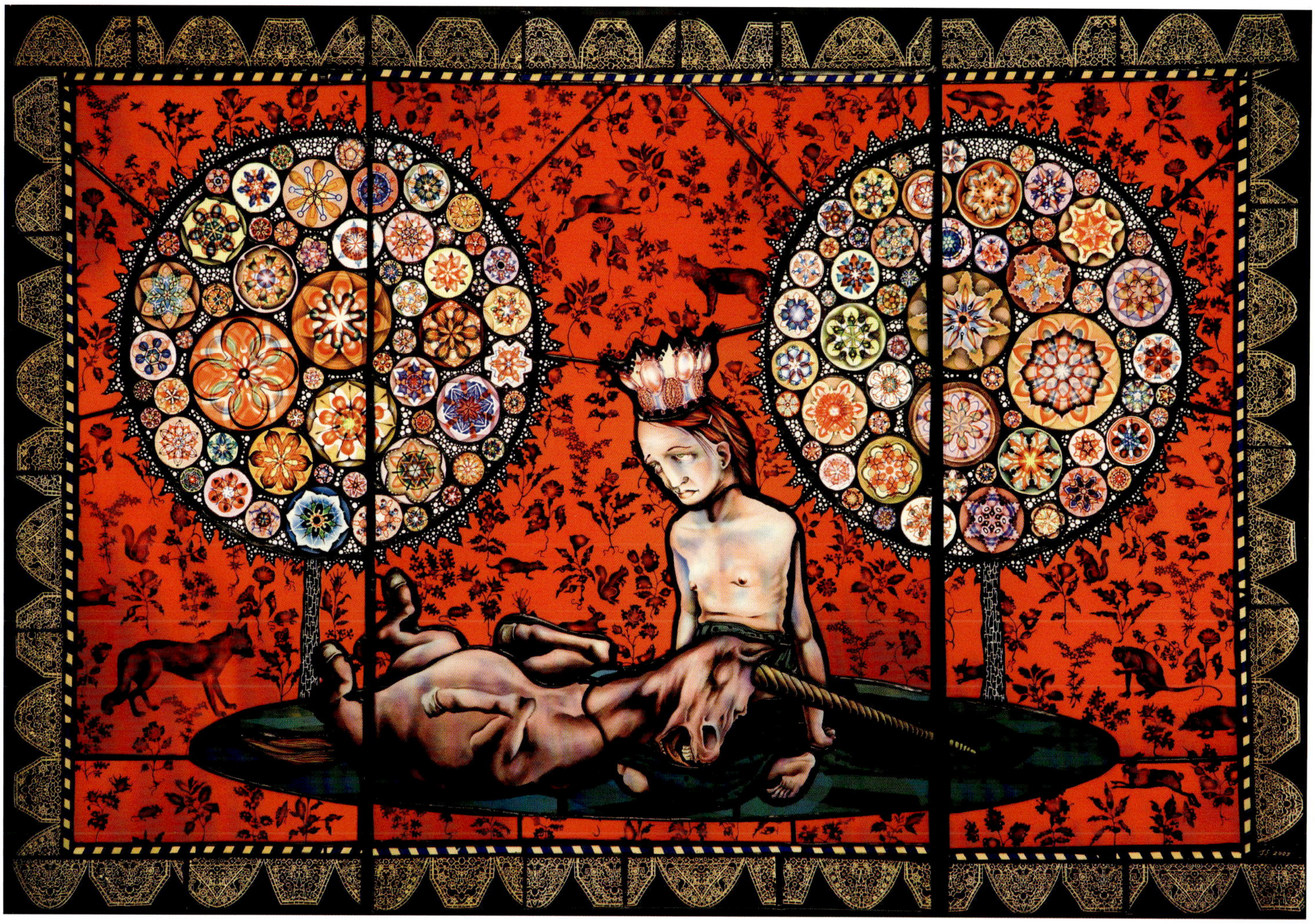

providing confidence that only the solid and settled seem able to portray. As Schaechter has pointed out, beauty is often about being full or complete, and subjects stuck in the netherworld of the in-between often seem nothing if not incomplete. By giving them a proper place, Schaechter has given them fullness, completeness, and yes, maybe even beauty. She has settled restless, wandering souls. She has anchored weary travelers. She has guided lost ships in the night. Judith Schaechter has pointed the way toward a new perception of the world and in doing so has illuminated the harsh contrasts that in the end create the most glorious light.

ANDREW WAGNER

(following pages)

Fig. 47
***Widow,* 2008, glass. Collection of Colleen and John Kotelly**

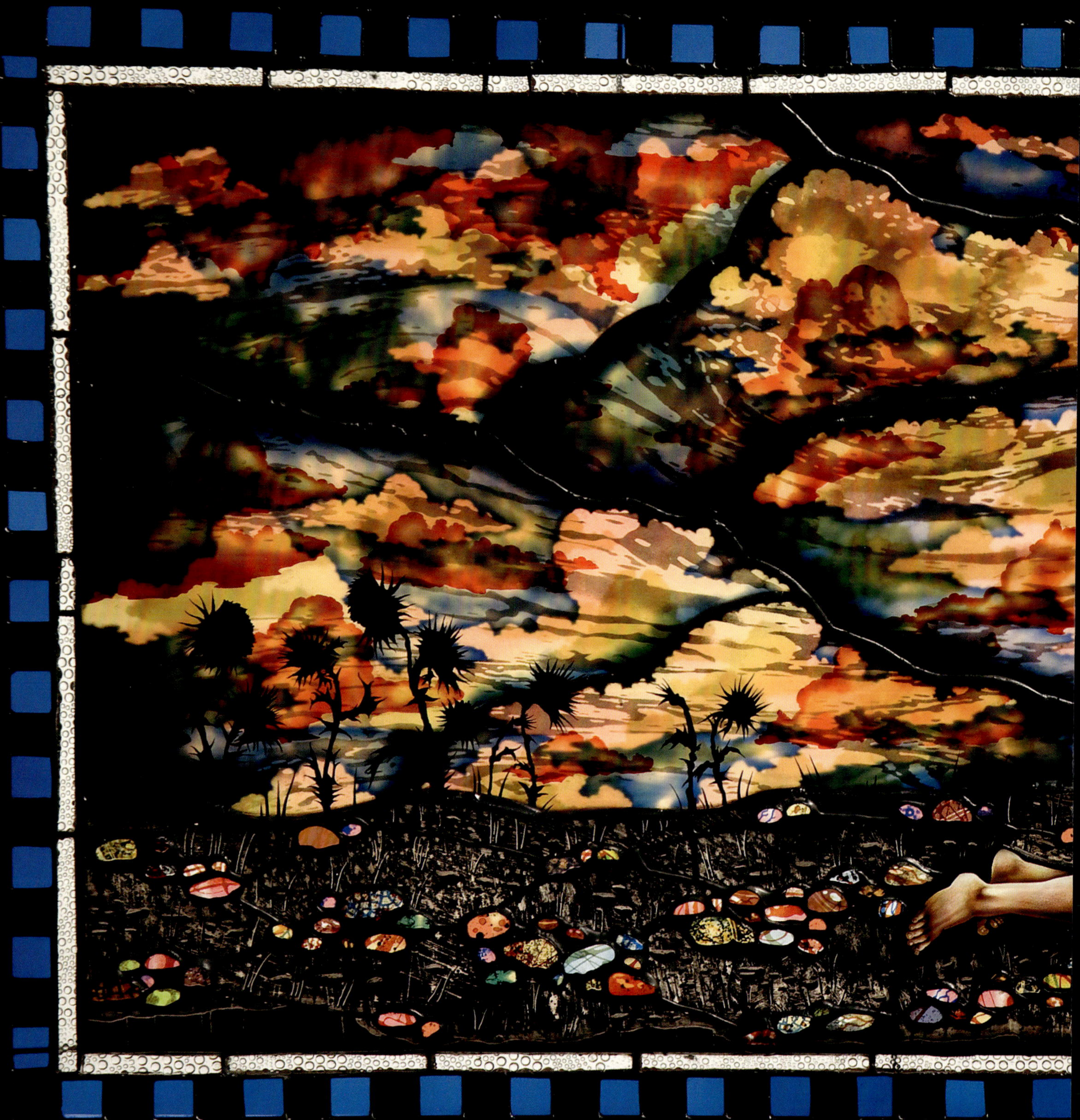

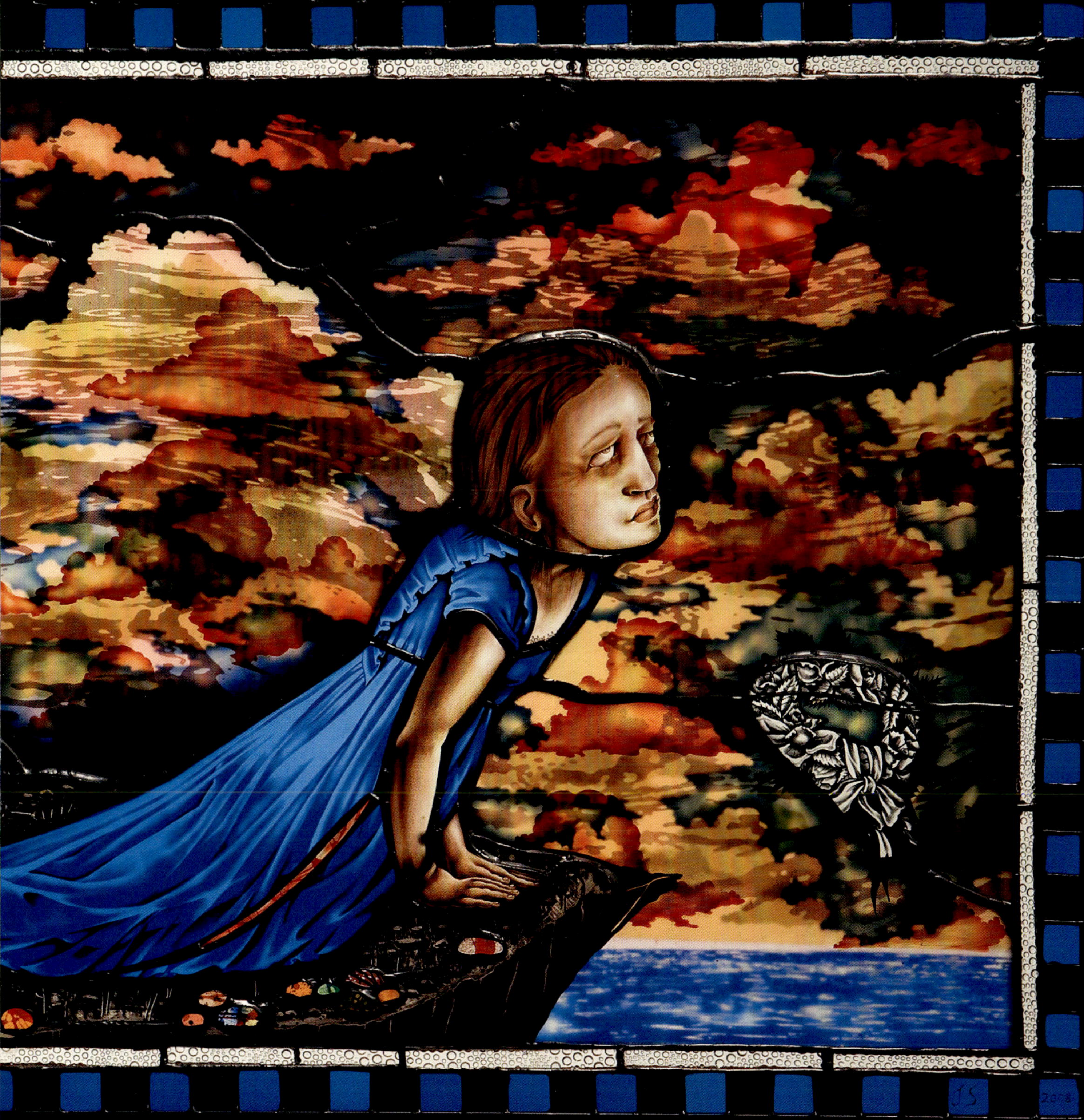
JS
2008

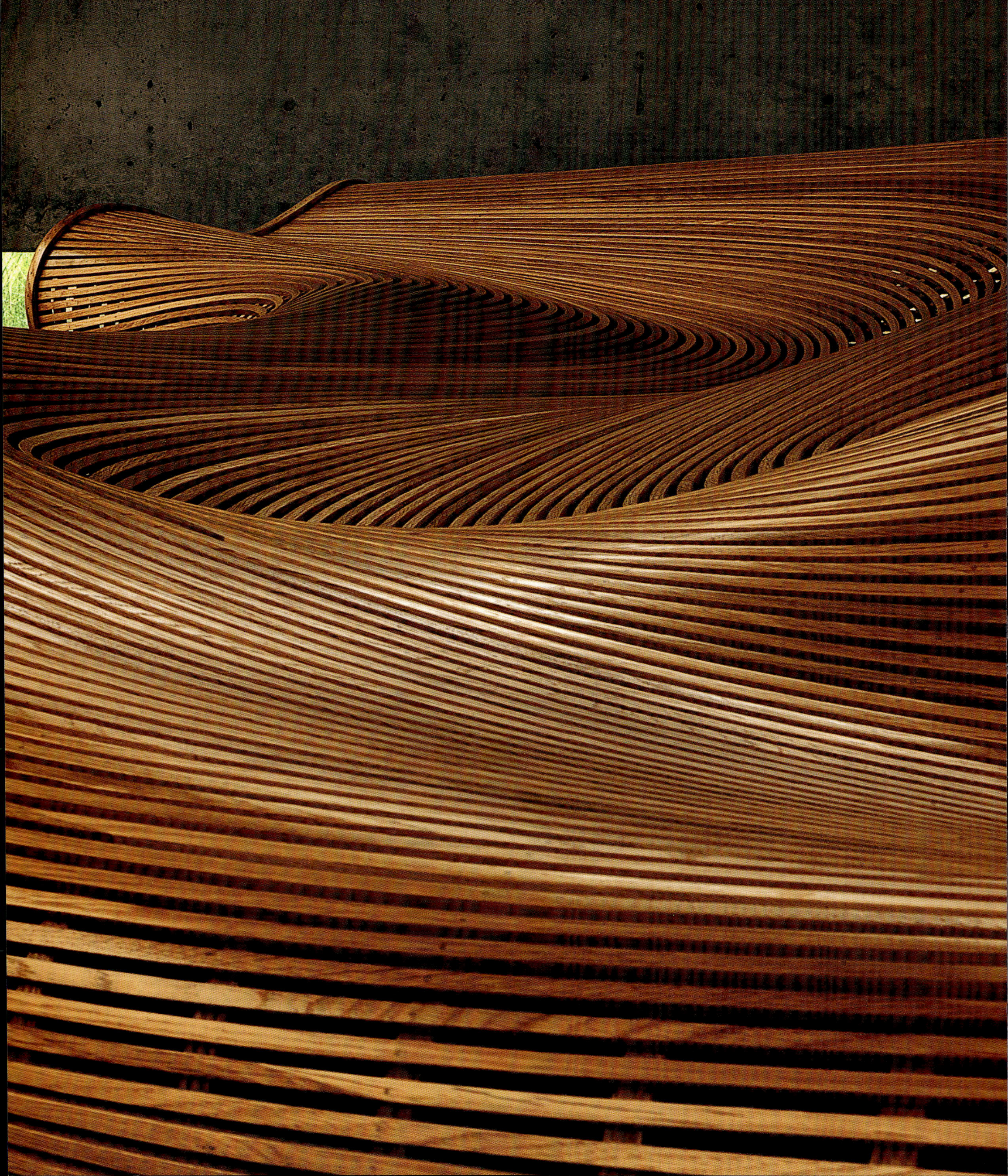

matthias pliessnig

One of the most extraordinary bodies of American furniture in recent memory developed out of a deceptively simple question: how do you build a boat? In the summer of 2006, Matthias Pliessnig, then a graduate student in the wood program at the University of Wisconsin–Madison, was in the department's shop when an engineering student approached him for assistance with his own boat project, inspired by the city's geography. Madison fills an isthmus pinched between Lakes Mendota and Monona—small bodies of water by Wisconsin standards but a force that laps constantly at the capital and looms in its psyche. Pliessnig was intrigued by the boat's spartan design—what he perceived as the "purity" of its form and function—and by the opportunity to investigate the boat-building process, and its obvious reward. He quickly convinced

Amada **(detail), 2010 (see pp. 86–87)**

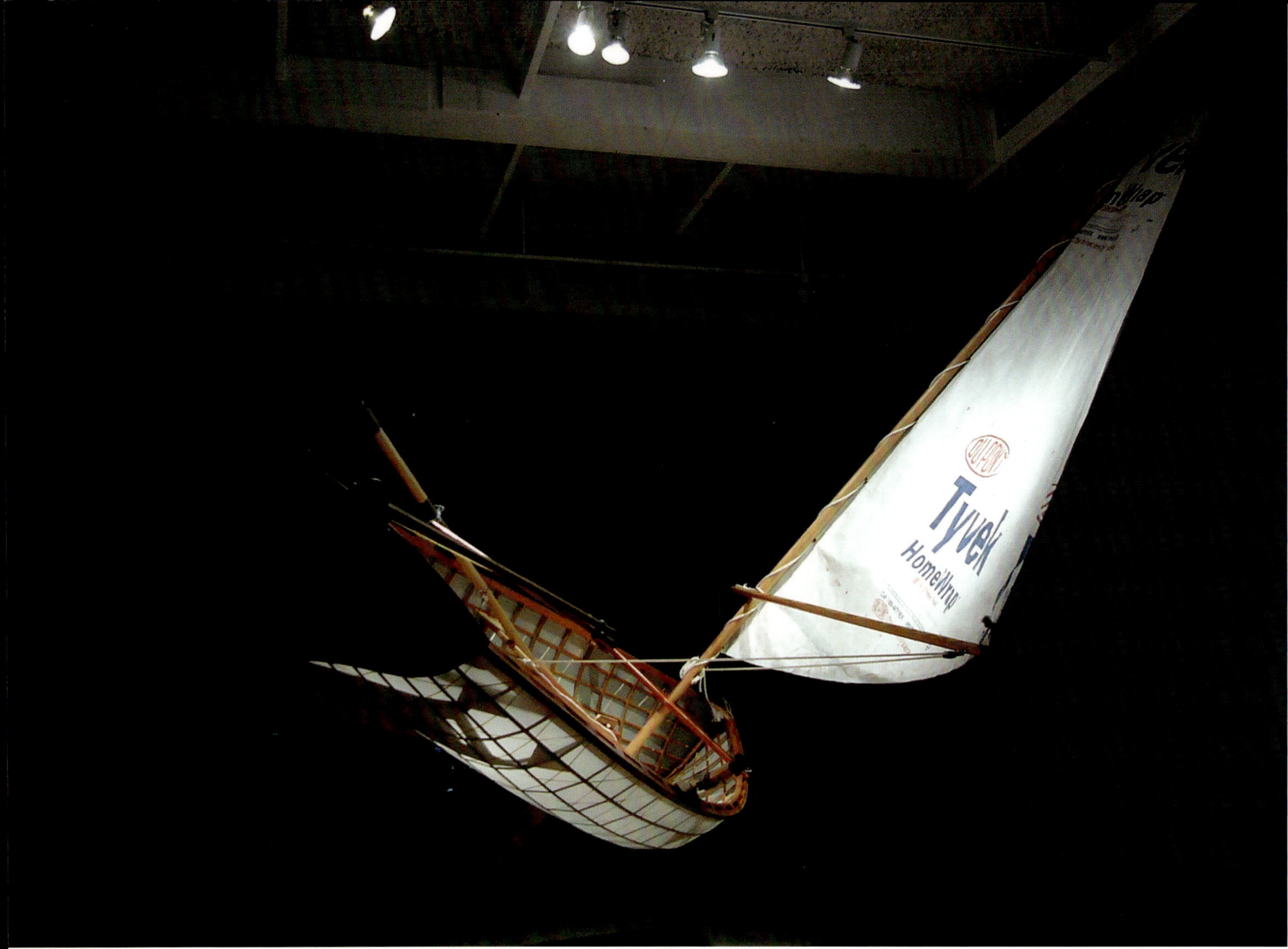

Fig. 48
***Classic 12* sailboat, 2006. Designed by Platt Monfort, Monfort and Associates, constructed by Matthias Pliessnig, white oak, fir, Kevlar roving, Dacron, Tyvek. Collection of the artist**

department head Tom Loeser and fellow graduate student Benjamin Wooten of the project's desirability, and each began construction of a simple craft: the Platt Monfort–designed *Classic 12* skiff (fig. 48).[27] Equipped with plans and basic kits, they muddled through the beginning stages of a centuries-old process.[28]

The traditional wooden boat's basic structure comprises stations and stringers. Stations are ribs that frame the craft's ultimate form by marking the width and depth of the vessel at regular intervals. Stringers connect the stations by running from bow to stern, securing them, and fleshing out the hull. Both components are steam bent to achieve their desired form. Strips of wood are first air dried, then soaked in water for several hours before being placed in a steam box, in this instance a high-temperature gauge PVC tube capped at both ends. The tube is inclined at a few degrees with a steam element at the lower end so that steam floods the enclosed space and passes out through a small hole at the high end. In this fashion, the wood is both saturated with water and heated, rendering the resin inside pliable and the wood extremely malleable. When the wood is removed, it must be bent into position and clamped into place within thirty seconds, after which it will cool, regaining rigidity. During this finite window the wood fibers will slip around one another to meet the stock's new form, allowing the wood to maintain its original strength (as opposed to sawn wood, in which the fibers are cut and weakened). After remaining clamped in position for six to eight hours the wood will maintain its new shape permanently.

The epiphany came six weeks later as Pliessnig sat in the boat of his making on Lake Mendota. The steam-bending process he had just experimented with could also be used to model a new type of furniture. While vital to marine design, steam bending's role in the history of furniture has been irregular, responsible for only isolated bursts of creativity, such as the eighteenth-century development of the Windsor chair, the "elastic" chairs of Samuel Gragg (1772–1855), and the immense catalogue of the Austrian firm Gebrüder Thonet in the second half of the nineteenth century. Innovative use of the technique since the twentieth century has proven elusive in the face of the widespread popularity of laminated wood products that negate the need to bend whole stock.

For Pliessnig, these disparate histories of craftsmanship would provide fuel for a new body of work, one uniquely tailored to his background. Pliessnig's undergraduate education was split between two

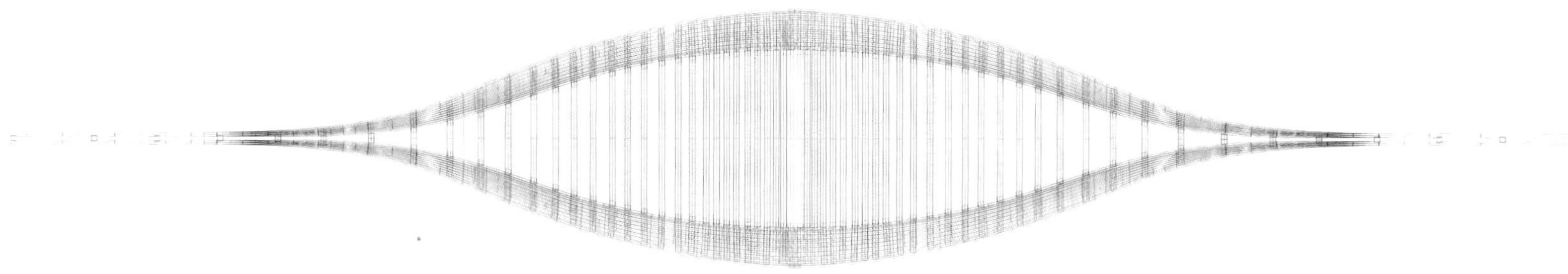

Fig. 49
Computer model for *Deviated Path,* 2006. Collection of the artist

Fig. 50
***Bends,* 2006, white oak. Courtesy of Lewis Wexler, Wexler Gallery, Philadelphia**

distinct departments at different institutions—sculpture at the Kansas City Art Institute, followed by furniture design at the Rhode Island School of Design (RISD). Between them he developed a happy equilibrium between conceptual and process-oriented approaches to craft, and a willingness to tackle complex issues of design. A series of wooden boxes constructed using advanced coopering techniques exhibits a highly original aesthetic and an early interest in challenging the physical capabilities of his materials. Two works from 2003, *Shell* and *Span,* illustrate Pliessnig's abiding interest in engineering. In each case a sleek wooden span rises between cast concrete footers, forming a bench resembling a bridge.[29] All furniture must take into account dynamic loads, yet Pliessnig focuses intently on the engineering aspect of his work, considering each piece a form of miniature architecture for the sitter's body.

This technical perspective broadened the scope of tools that could be employed in the conceptualization of new work—chief among them, Rhinoceros 3-D modeling software. As Pliessnig considered a body of furniture founded on the principles of marine design, Rhino offered the ability to produce advanced drawings, critical to a project employing unfamiliar techniques. The plan for *Deviated Path,* 2006, Pliessnig's first work following the skiff, exhibits the degree to which that building exercise captivated his imagination (fig. 49). The piece resembles a hull upturned to act as a bench, with its center depressed to cradle the sitter. At fourteen feet in length, it was also long enough for the wood to gently curve without the aid of steam. Other works followed in quick succession. *Bends* (fig. 50) and *Convolution* of 2006 and *Waive,* 2007,

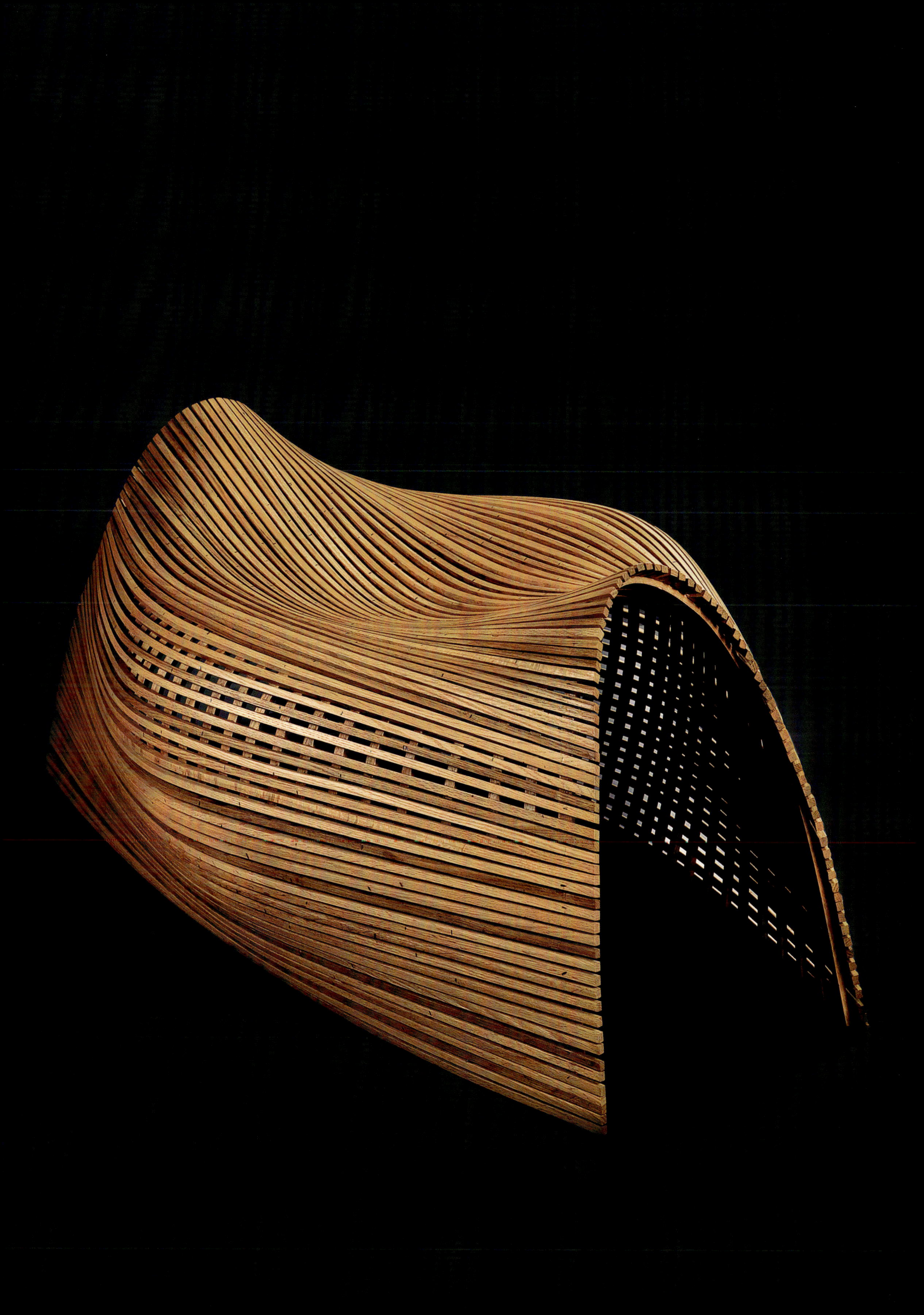

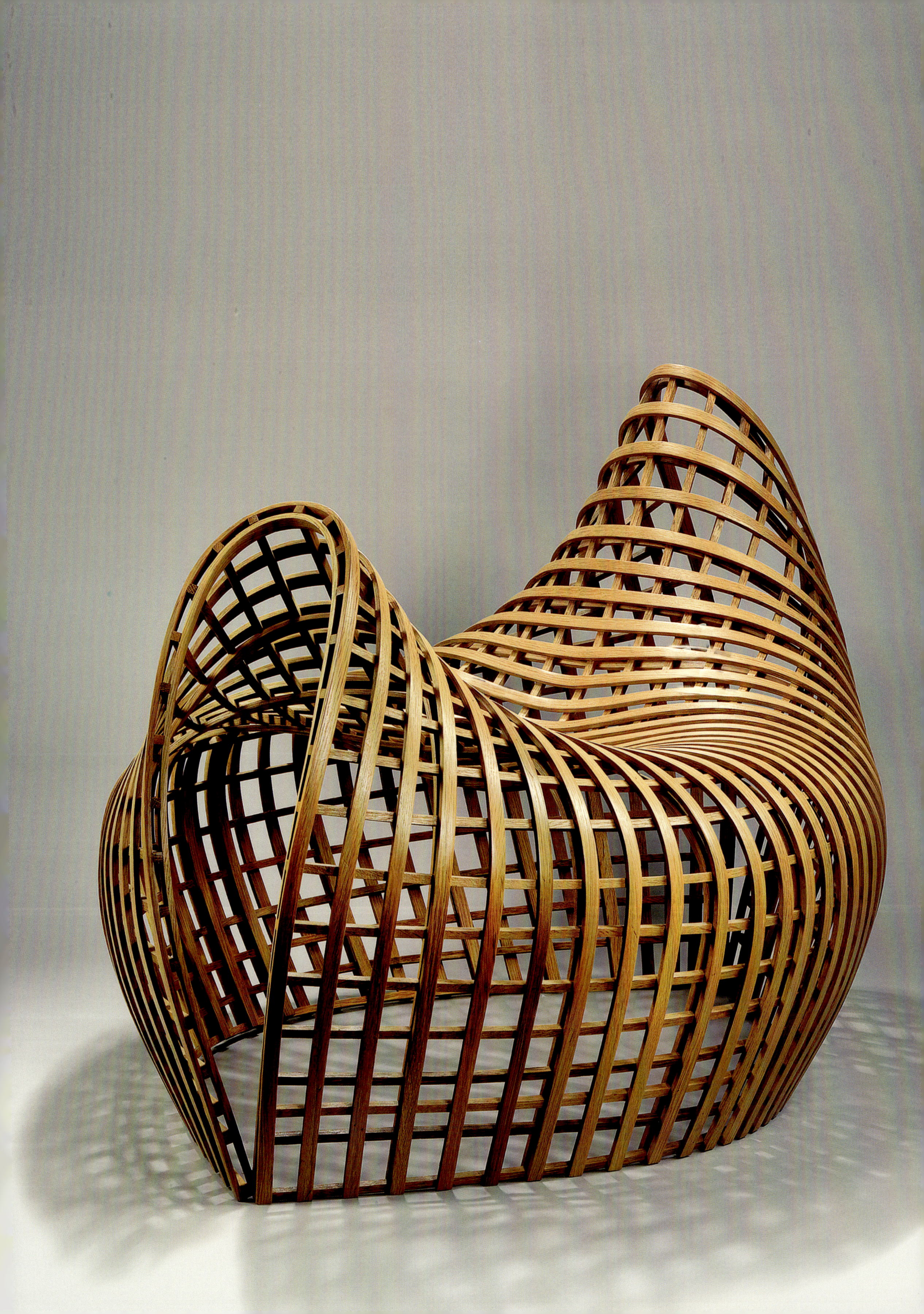

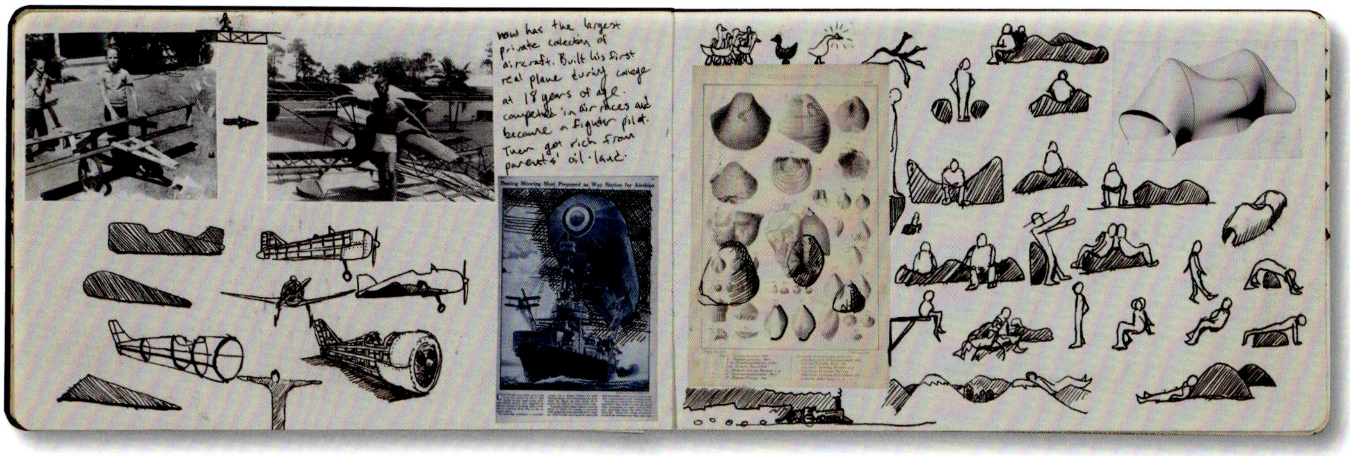

(fig. 51) demonstrated not only the aesthetics but also the mechanics of traditional boat-building. Evident in each piece is Pliessnig's first use of stations, stringers, and steam bending to achieve a final form. While the function of each work is suggested by a central depression for seating, their overall effect is far more sculptural than that of the comparably conservative *Deviated Path.* Thin ribs of white oak bulge, dip, and swoop around the would-be sitter, suggesting more organic influences than the rigid design of boats.

Pages from Pliessnig's sketchbooks reveal the development of this more gestural style, influenced in part by his study of ergonomics (fig. 52). He draws figures in white space, performing myriad actions—sitting, standing, walking, leaning—before sketching in solid forms to support them. The first evidence of what Pliessnig has referred to as the "landscape for the body" appears here, as furniture contours to the subject's every whim.[30] This reverse design approach would eventually allow Pliessnig to break free from the final restriction placed on his work by marine design—its obligatory symmetry—and to fully explore wood's plasticity.

Fig. 51
***Waive,* 2007, white oak. Collection of Lorraine W. Hilleman**

Fig. 52
Sketches from the artist's sketchbook, 2010, bound paper. Collection of the artist

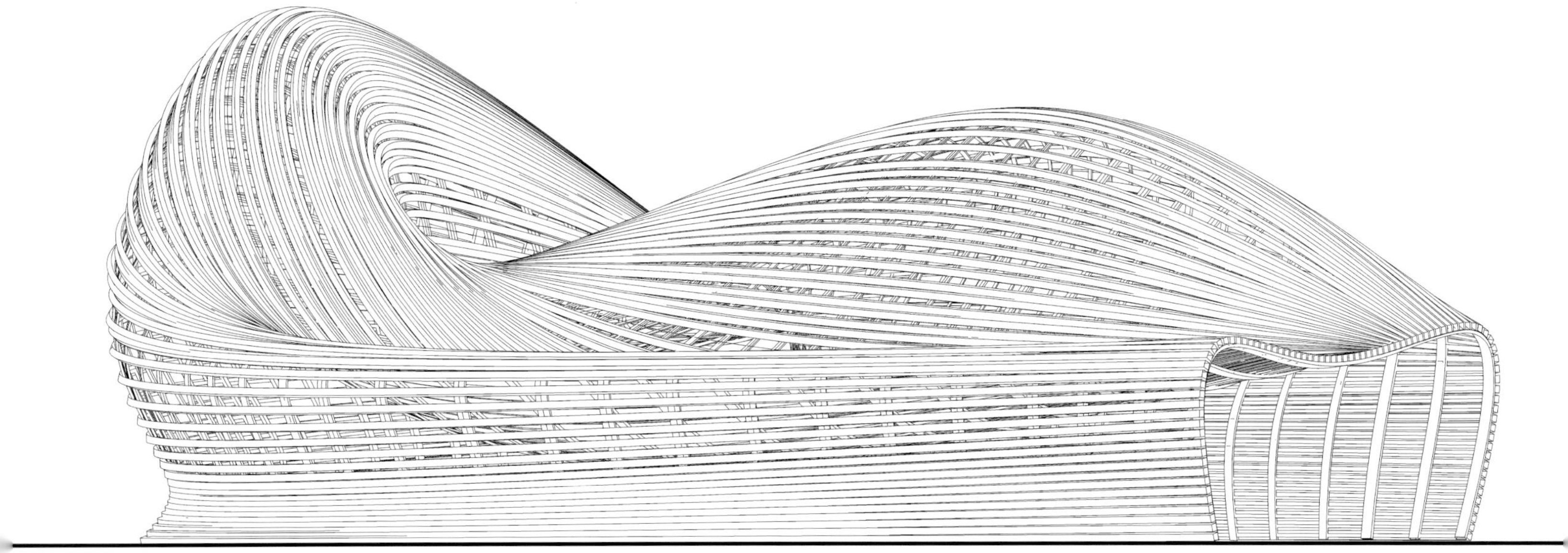

Fig. 53
Computer model for *Providence*, 2008. Collection of the artist

Fig. 54
Computer model for *Drift*, 2010. Collection of the artist

Matthias Pliessnig's growing comfort with process and material is revealed in his first multiseat work, *Providence,* 2008 (fig. 53). Named after the capital of Rhode Island (and home to RISD), *Providence* bends and twists two primary seating areas around a central arc framed by two peaks that mimic the city's topography. Between them a valley of complex compound curves unfolds into separate areas for repose that employ the peaks as seatbacks. With more than seven thousand points of contact, the sheer scale and physicality of *Providence* represents a leap in the maturity of Pliessnig's oeuvre. *Drift,* 2010, revisits this geometry but comes to a subtler conclusion: rather than bulging seatbacks and a sweeping footprint, a central rise meanders across a narrower body, suggesting an updated conversation sofa (fig. 54).

The shift to furniture made for more than one sitter presented challenges in the design and execution of increasingly complex work. Because 3-D modeling software cannot account for the restrictive properties of organic materials, Rhino evolved into a better tool for drafting ideas and later analyzing the geometry of the finished piece

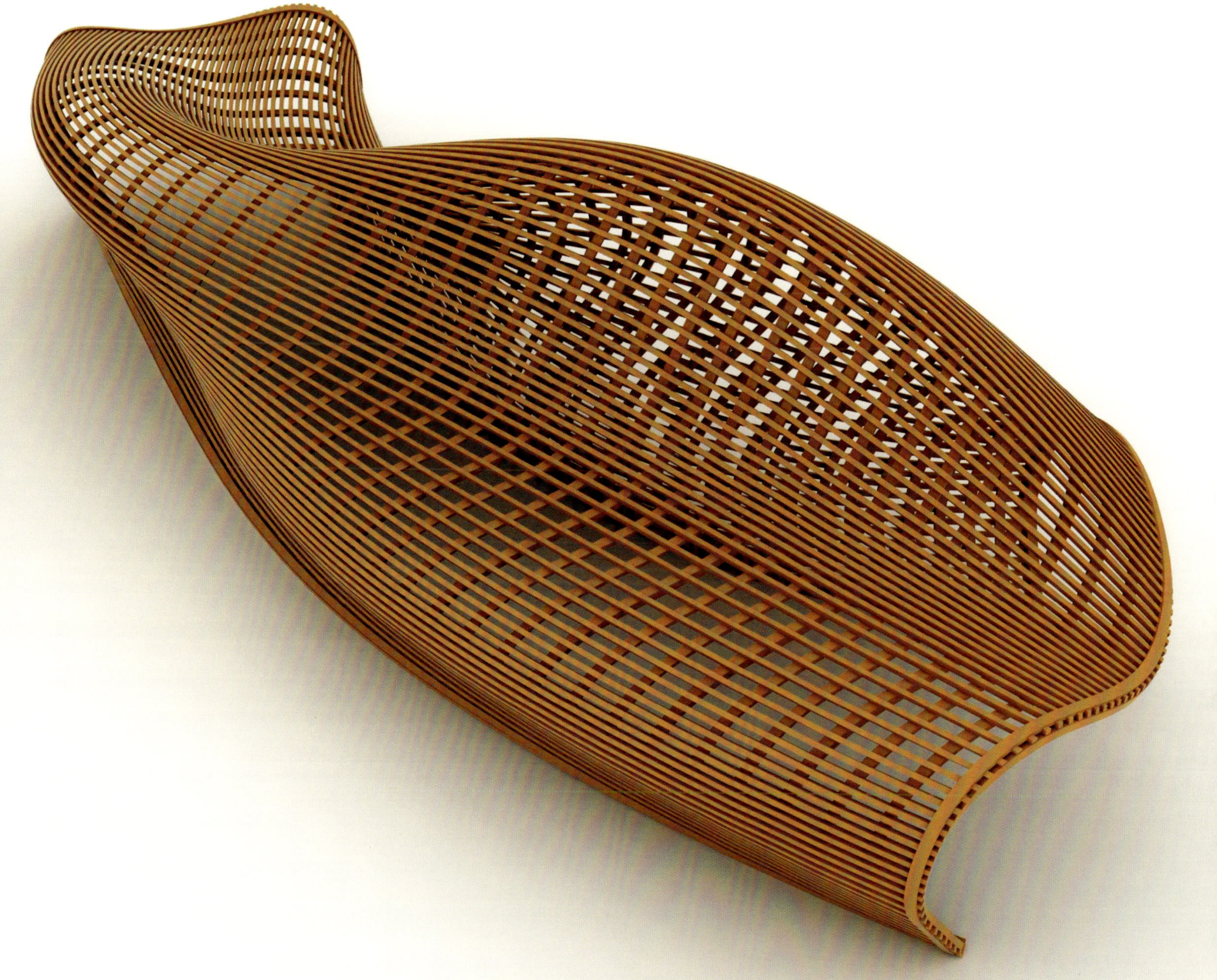

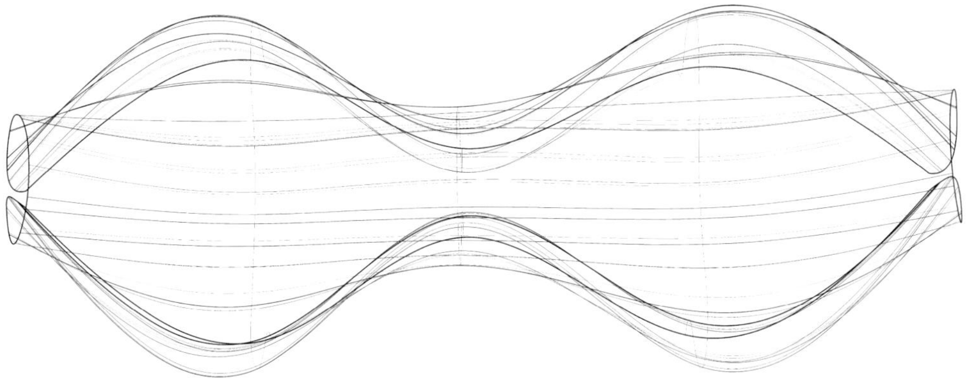

Fig. 55
Computer model for *Rivulet,* 2009. Collection of the artist

Fig. 56
***Rivulet,* 2009, white oak and bamboo. Private collection**

than for plotting each line as a guide for construction. The computer model for *Rivulet,* 2009, shows only five stations spaced out in a draft outline while a handful of stringers suggest the final form (fig. 55). The completed work illustrates how that design was altered during fabrication (fig. 56). Using sawn plywood stations and a few strategically placed stringers, Pliessnig is able to sketch out a work in real time. How the stock will respond to proposed curves is easily tested, and adjustments in design can be incorporated without great difficulty. Yet the window during which steamed wood can be manipulated never expands, necessitating an often frenetic pace of work as limp oak strips exit the steamer and are clamped into ever more advanced positions. Once set, the stringers are unclamped, the grain, which is raised in the steaming process, is sanded down, and each segment is affixed to the overall structure with marine epoxy. *Rivulet* in particular exhibits an obsessive level of craftsmanship: its stringers are sandwiched between two sets of stations, and each of the several thousand points of contact is pegged with bamboo.

Pliessnig's recent *Amada,* 2010, demonstrates the rapid sophistication of his technique and the capacity for his work to achieve astonishing scale (fig. 57). Three eight-foot lengths of white oak are joined together to create twenty-four-foot-long stringers and a form that breaks from the intuitive objecthood of its predecessors. While previous works revealed function through their human scale and their basic resemblance to a boat, chair, or bench, *Amada* surpasses recognizable markers in design, prevailing less as furniture than as a

(following pages)

Fig. 57
***Amada,* 2010, white oak. Private collection**

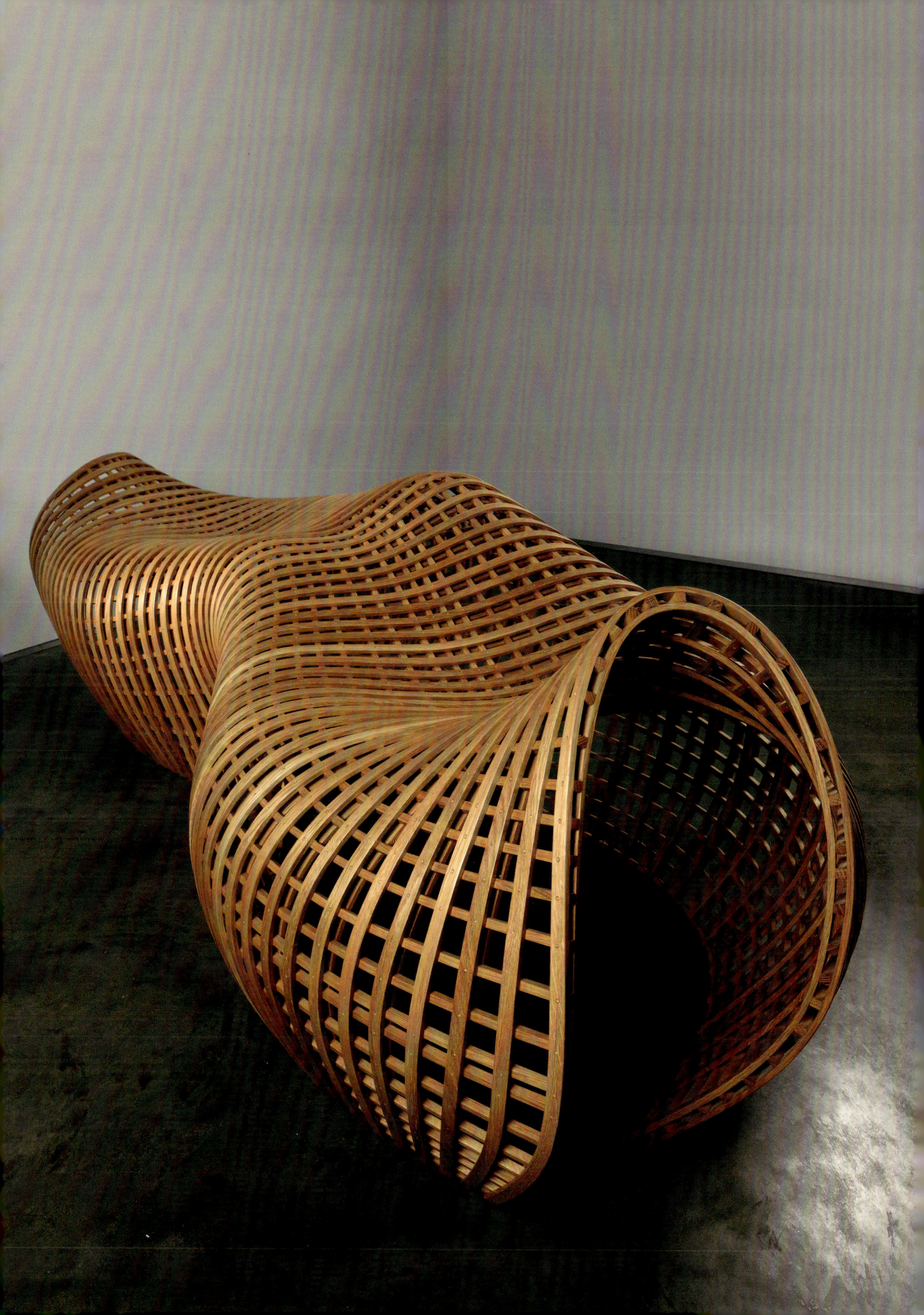

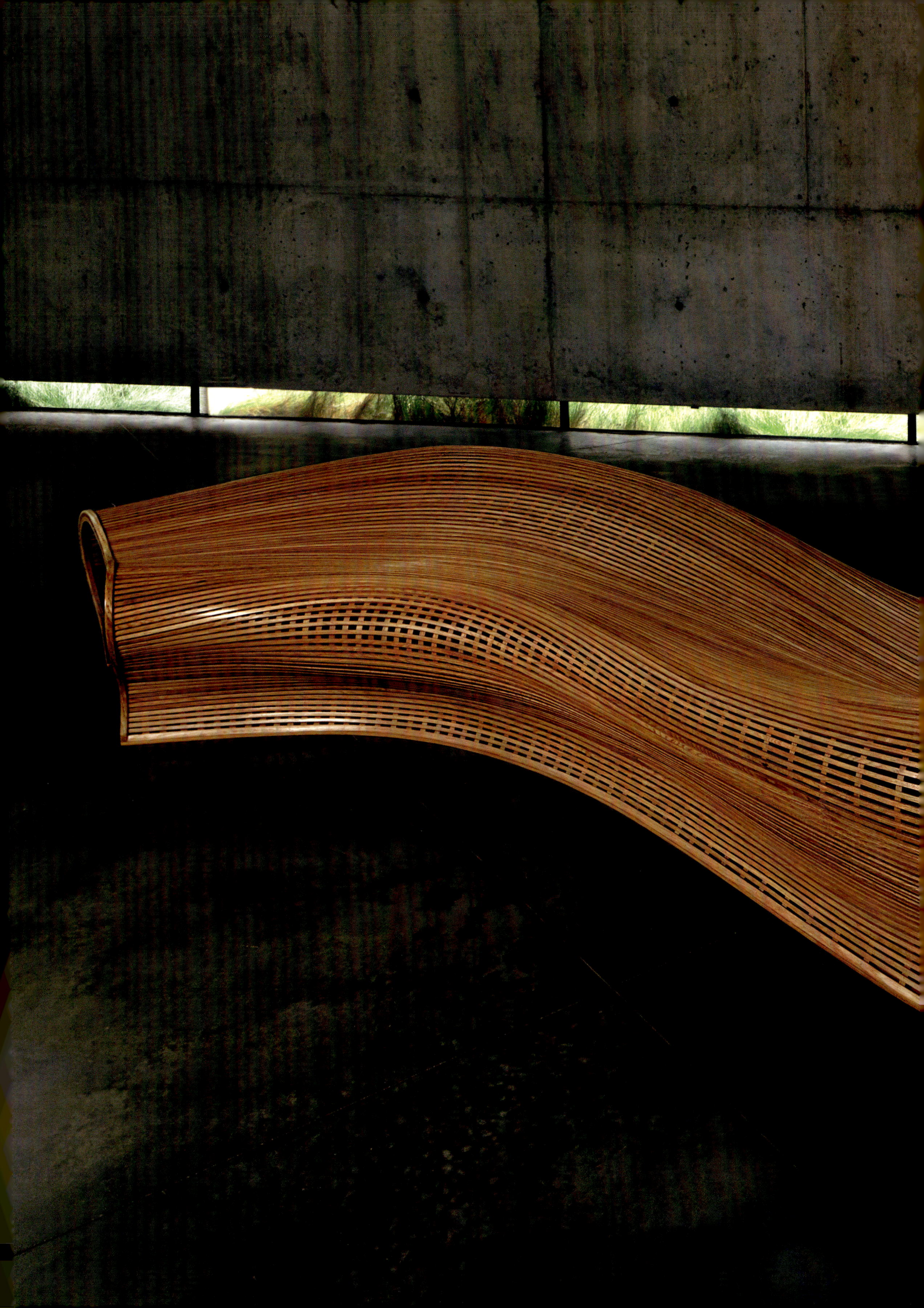

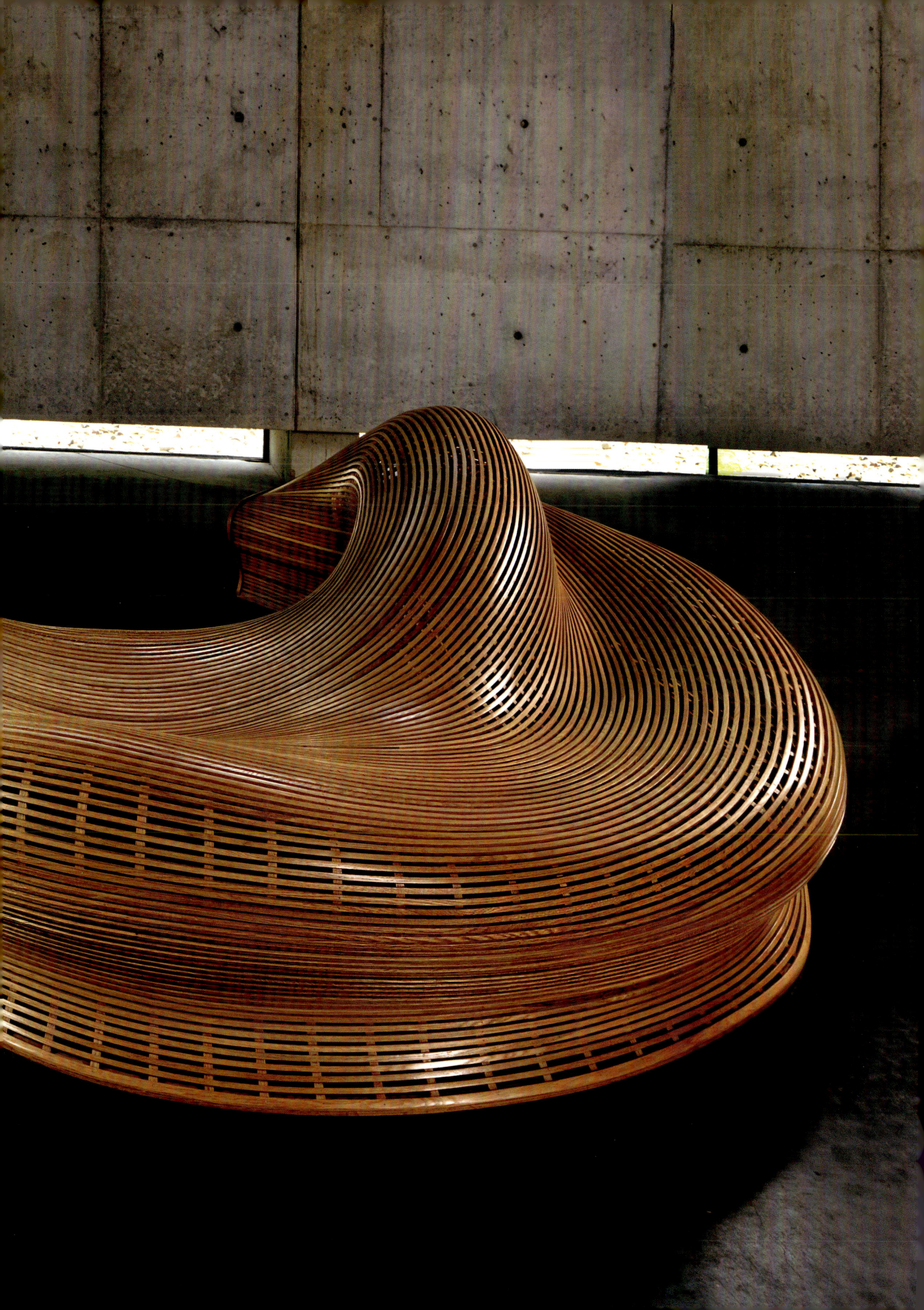

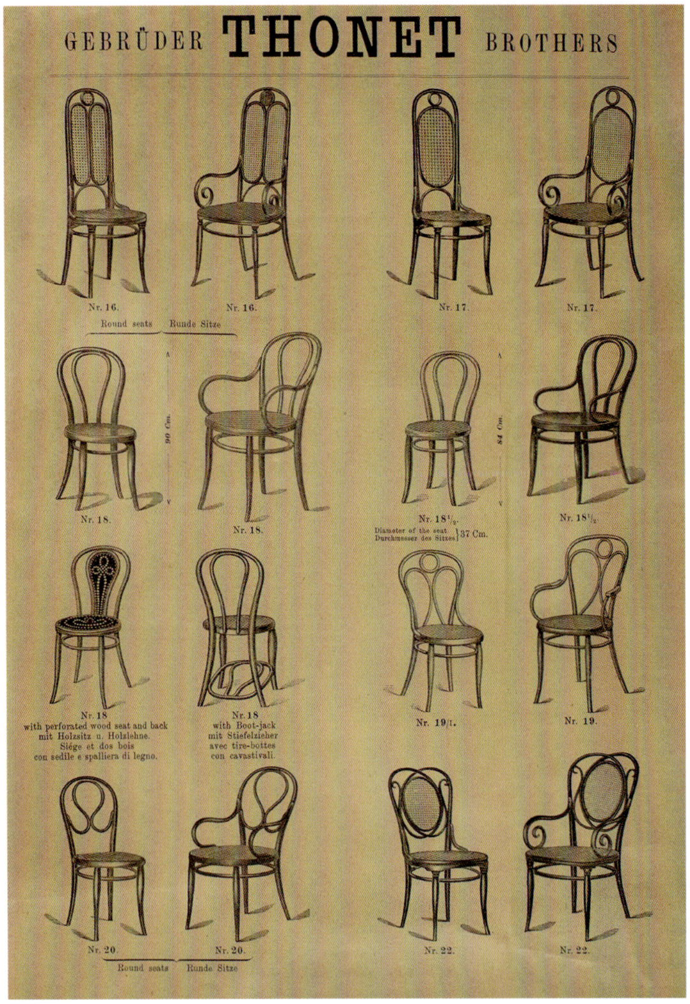

Fig. 58
Full page showing Thonet chairs nos. 16–22, from Gebrüder Thonet, *The Thonet Bent Wood Furniture* (Vienna, Austria; NewYork: Thonet Brothers, about 1886). Courtesy, The Winterthur Library, Printed Book and Periodical Collection

Fig. 59
***Thonet No. 18*, 2007, white oak and Thonet No. 18 café chair. Courtesy of Lewis Wexler, Wexler Gallery, Philadelphia**

sculptural environment. How to engage that environment is an open question: does one sit, stand, lie, or crawl among its folds?

Matthias Pliessnig's conceptual challenge to furniture is also revealed in his 2007 piece, *Thonet No. 18* (figs. 58, 59). In his only major work to date incorporating secondary materials, Pliessnig has wrapped every part of a found Thonet café chair in strips of white oak. It displays none of the careful planning or consideration of form exhibited in other works. The artist instead focused on the spontaneity of execution possible as wood exits the steamer.

Pliessnig is intensely interested in the history and design of Thonet furniture and the company's role in modernizing the steam-bending process. Michael Thonet (1796–1871) experimented with laminated, then bentwood, furniture techniques for decades, before patenting a process for bending solid wood in 1856. The chairs developed by Gebrüder Thonet from that date would revolutionize nineteenth- and early twentieth-century spaces through their clean lines, lightweight and durable construction, and uniformity of manufacture, achieved through a rigid factory production system. Introduced in 1876, the No. 18 chair ranked as one of Thonet's most popular models, inspiring many related designs and ensuring a lasting presence on the market (it remains in production today).

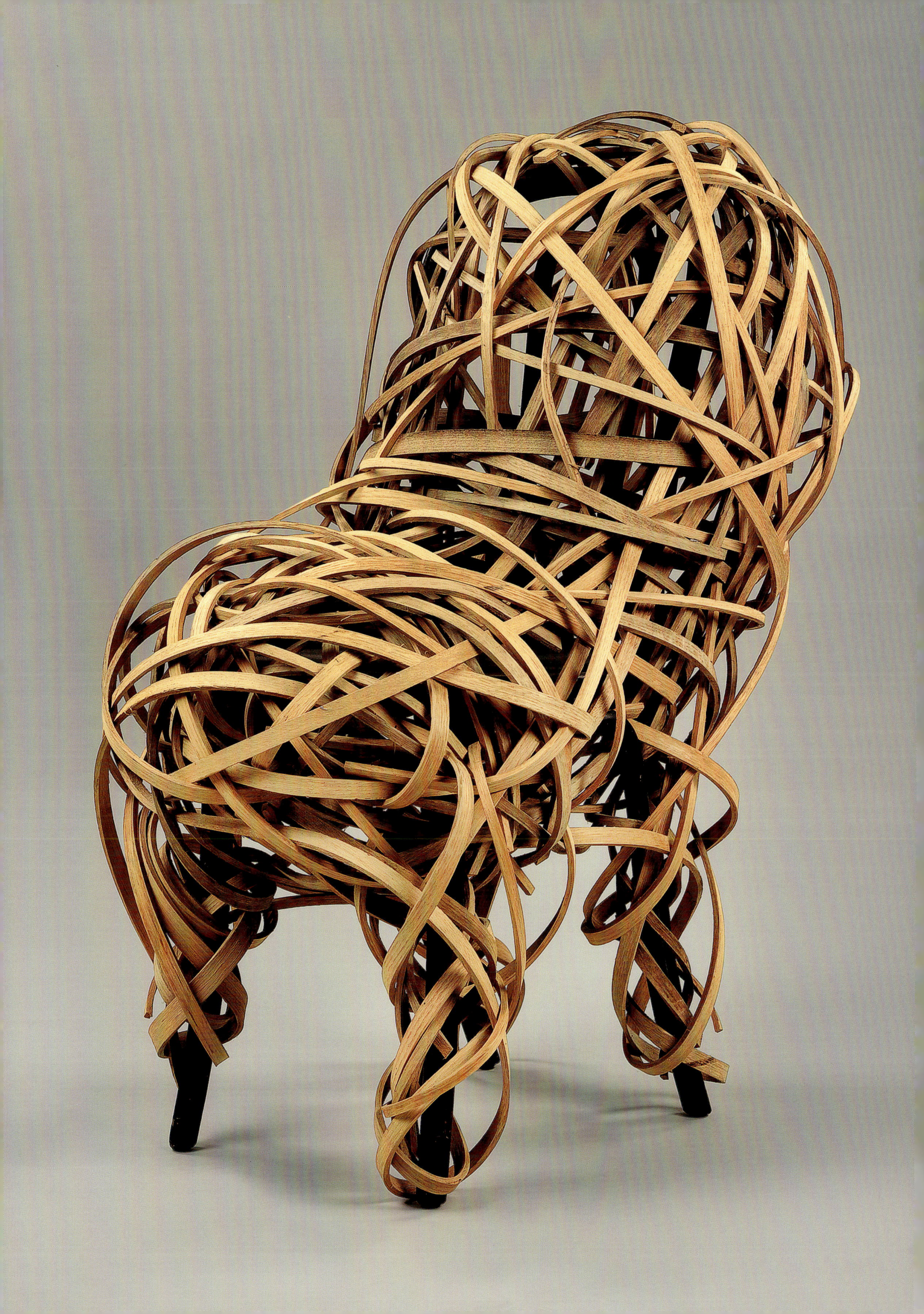

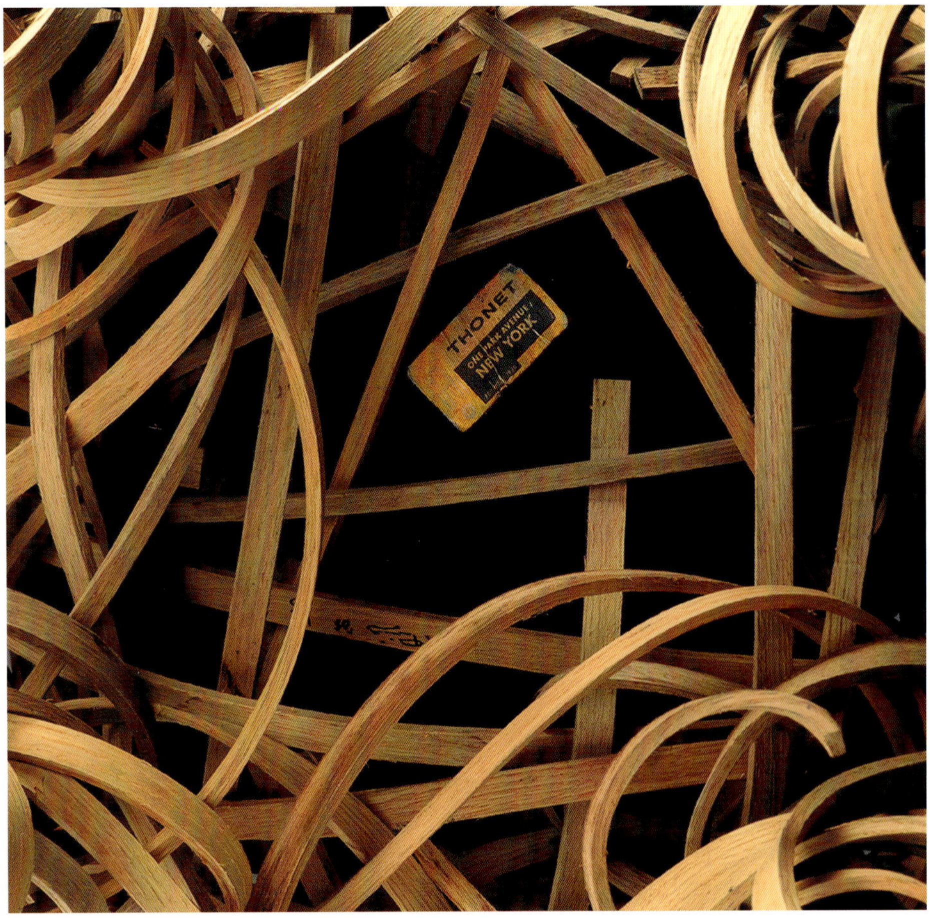

Thonet chairs' standardized manufacture, affordability, and ubiquity led them to become a symbol of nineteenth-century optimism surrounding the Industrial Revolution.

Pliessnig's tongue-in-cheek reappraisal provides a fitting bookend to the modern history of steam-bent furniture. The twisted strands of rough, unsanded oak render the chair unusable, creating instead a sculptural commentary on construction practices and craft's historical arc

***Thonet No. 18* (detail), 2007**

as a response to mass production. If bentwood café chairs can stand for the relentless progression of industry and its impact on material life, then this chair is a bespoke footnote, reminding us of a viable alternative.

In the span of five years, Matthias Pliessnig has reinvigorated contemporary American furniture practice through his insatiable curiosity, unexpected approach to design, and fervent dedication to craftsmanship. The question going forward is how this young artist will continue to impact multiple fields through his work, which happily blurs the lines between design, craft, sculpture, and engineering. The swift progression in scale from *Bends* to *Amada,* and in content from a simple skiff to the twisted message in *Thonet No. 18,* belies the ambition of future projects. Pliessnig has already expressed an interest in testing the viability of steam-bent wood as a major architectural component. If boats and furniture can be viewed as basic protectors from water and earth, then perhaps buildings, our shelter from the elements, are a natural subject in a continuing investigation of the primary functions of material culture. It is a connection Pliessnig is determined to make, one stringer at a time.

NICHOLAS R. BELL

notes

1. Even today, only his shop is entrusted with filling orders for these.

2. The influence of life casting on rococo silver, as well as its process, was covered extensively in an essay Vitali wrote for Sotheby's auction house when it auctioned off the Thyssen Meissonnier tureen in May 1998 (see n. 4 below). The essay was titled "Meissonnier's Goldsmith Persona: A Sublimation of Forms and Techniques, *Natura ed Invenzione*" and ran seventeen pages, with twenty-eight illustrations.

3. A selection of Vitali's writings is included in the bibliography at the back of this catalogue. He has also written an essay entitled "The Master and the Masterpiece: An Enquiry into the Goldsmith's Influences and Intentions during his Creative Process" for a forthcoming book on the Toledo (Ohio) Museum of Art's celebrated European silver collection.

4. A private collector paid more than $5.7 million at auction for the tureen. Interestingly enough, Vitali considers that liner one of his finest pieces of modern design.

5. Vitali, quoted in Jennifer Olshin, "A Renaissance Man of Metalwork," *New York Times*, December 5, 1999.

6. The tureen was commissioned specifically for use in serving a *risotto alla pescatora*, and the form was meant to evoke a fisherman's boat as well as ocean waves.

7. This was in a one-person exhibition in the Contemporary Craft Gallery at the Newark Museum, 1990. To date, Vitali has made seven versions of this tureen. The same year that Houston ordered its version, Heinrich von Thyssen Jr. ordered a pair of the same form.

8. Betty Freudenheim, "Evoking Silver's Magical Power," *New York Times*, December 2, 1990.

9. The couple, Iris and Seymour Schwartz, purchased the Texas centerpiece after the original commissioners rejected it.

10. Initially the Vitali pieces were showcased in a Movado store in the Mall at Short Hills, New Jersey. Movado gave a coffeepot of this form to the Newark Museum in 1999; after Vitali's relationship with Movado ended, a second full service was ordered by Ricardo and Janet Zapata of Short Hills, New Jersey, to mark their twenty-fifth wedding anniversary.

11. The exhibition, *Lions, Dragons and Other Beasts: Aquamanilia of the Middle Ages, Vessels for Church and Table*, opened at the Bard Center for Studies in the Decorative Arts, Design and Culture, in New York in 2006.

12. All quotes are by Cliff Lee in conversation with the author, Stevens, Pennsylvania, 18 September 2009.

13. Chen Baiquan, "The Development of Song Dynasty Qingbai wares in Jingdezhen," in *The Porcelains of Jingdezhen*, ed. Rosemary E. Scott (London: University of London, Percival David Foundation of Chinese Art, 1993), 18–19. For an example of molding without carving, see a fourteenth-century Longquan ware baluster-shaped vase in Yutaka Mino and Katherine R. Tsiang, *Ice and Green Clouds: Traditions of Chinese Celadon* (Indianapolis: Indianapolis Museum of Art; Bloomington: Indiana University Press, 1986), 200.

14. In theatrical productions based on the novel, the costume of the shepherd, Celadon, always included grayish green ribbons. We are indebted to nineteenth-century French collectors for baptizing Song wares with the term. Robert Finlay, *The Pilgrim Art: Cultures of Porcelain in World History* (Berkeley: University of California Press, 2010), 133. See also Sarah Richards, *Eighteenth-Century Ceramics: Products for a Civilised Society* (Manchester, UK: Manchester University Press, 1999), 202–3.

15. "Chicken fat" and "tender yellow" were common Chinese descriptors for the glaze's color. Nigel Wood, *Chinese Glazes: Their Origins, Chemistry, and Recreation* (London: A & C Black; Philadelphia: University of Pennsylvania Press, 1999), 244.

16. Nigel Wood, "The Evolution of Chinese Copper Red," in *Chinese Copper Red Wares*, ed. Rosemary E. Scott (London: University of London, Percival David Foundation of Chinese Art, 1992), 11, 27–28.

17. Percival David Foundation of Chinese Art, *Illustrated Catalogue of Ru, Guan, Jun, Guandong, and Yixing Wares in the Percival David Foundation of Chinese Art* (London: University of London, Percival David Foundation of Chinese Art, 1999), 6–8. *Ru* ware remains one of the scarcest surviving Chinese porcelains. Fittingly, the largest extant collection resides at Taipei's National Palace Museum, where it would have been accessible to a young Cliff Lee.

18. Wood, *Chinese Glazes*, 137.

19. For a description of how "hare's fur" develops during firing, see ibid., 149. See also Robert D. Mowry et al., *Hare's Fur, Tortoiseshell, and Partridge Feathers: Chinese Brown- and Black-Glazed Ceramics, 400–1400* (Cambridge, MA: Harvard Art Museums, 1996).

20. For an early example of the snakeskin effect, see an eighteenth-century tea bowl from Aira town, Japan, in the collection of the Freer Gallery of Art, F1911.379.

21. Unless otherwise noted, quotes by the artist are from a lecture Judith Schaechter gave at the Observatory Room, Brooklyn, New York, on 5 June 2010.

22. Robert Sullivan, "Through the Looking Glass," *American Craft* 69, no. 1 (February/March 2009): 66.

23. Ibid.

24. Interview between the author and Judith Schaechter, posted to YouTube on 6 November 2009, http:///youtube.com/watch?v=aCoCmFaJ0ek&feature=related, accessed 4 October 2010 (hereafter cited as Schaechter interview). Transcript of video interview on file in the Smithsonian American Art Museum curatorial files.

25. Schaechter interview.

26. Quoted in Sullivan, "Through the Looking Glass," 64–66.

27. For more information on Platt Monfort's boat designs, including the *Classic 12*, visit Geodesic Aerolite Boats at www.gaboats.com.

28. In the spring of 2005, before Pliessnig's enrollment, Wisconsin boatbuilder Joshua W. Swan served as artist-in-residence at the University of Wisconsin–Madison department of art. With the aid of Loeser and students interested in boat-building, he constructed a thirteen-and-a-half-foot-frame Maine Peapod on the seventh floor of the department, leading to the workshop title "The Boatyard in the Sky." Swan was a source of advice and encouragement during the impromptu building session in 2006.

29. See John Kelsey, ed. *Furniture Makers Explore Digital Technologies*, Furniture Studio Series (Free Union, VA: Furniture Society, 2005), 57.

30. Matthias Pliessnig in conversation with the author, Philadelphia, 29 October 2009.

ubaldo vitali

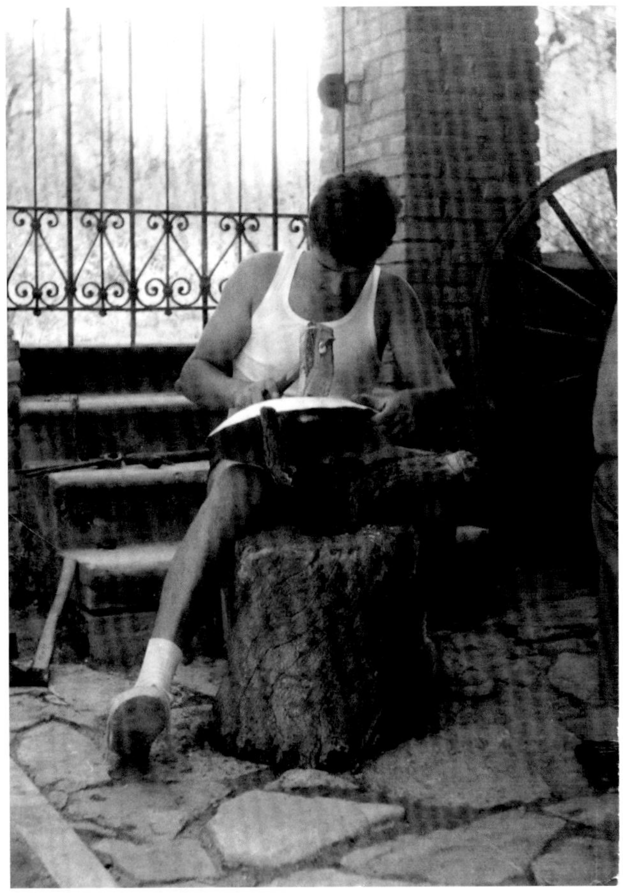

Born in 1944 and raised in Rome, Ubaldo Vitali is a fourth-generation silversmith who learned the craft from his father and grandfather. Vitali studied drawing, painting, sculpture, and art history in Rome at the Liceo Artistico Ripetta, architecture at the Università di Roma, and sculpture at the Accademia di Belle Arti, where he met his future wife, Anita, who is American. He immigrated to the United States in 1967 and set up a studio in Belleville, New Jersey, near a Tiffany & Co. silver factory.

A master craftsman in silver and gold, Vitali is also a restorer, conservator, scholar, and sculptor. He has done extensive work for companies such as Tiffany, Bulgari, Cartier, Steuben, and Movado, as well as for auction houses, museums, and private collectors. Vitali has also executed commissions for popes, kings, queens, and American presidents. He has written several articles for magazines on historical practices, such as lost-wax casting, and essays for exhibition catalogues. Vitali has been featured in many museum exhibits, including one at the Newark Museum in 1990; he made a number of objects in collaboration with Leonard DiNardo. Vitali's work is in several museum collections, including the Museum of Fine Arts, Houston, TX, and the Yale University Art Gallery, New Haven, CT. His workshop is in Maplewood, New Jersey.

cliff lee

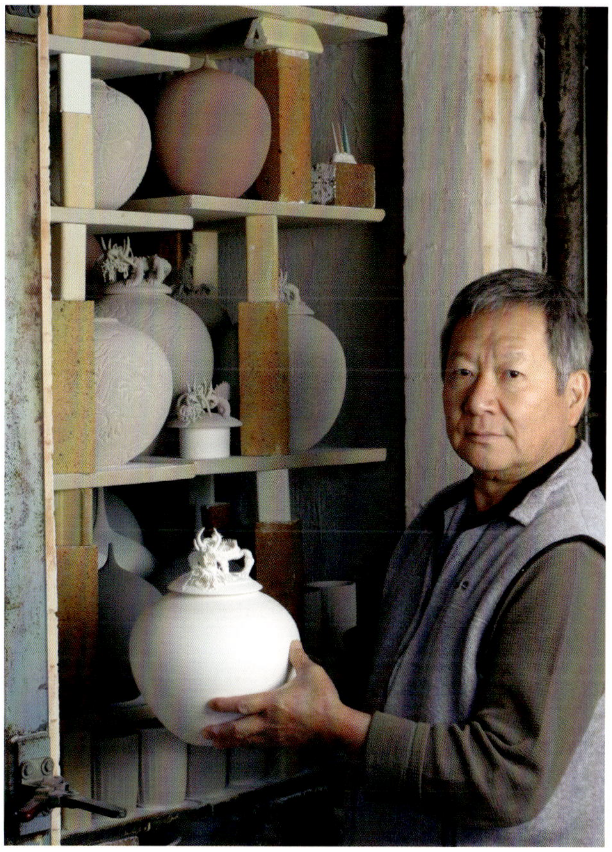

Cliff Lee was born in Vienna, Austria, in 1951, where his father was stationed as ambassador. Lee began his education in Taiwan and moved to the United States in 1968 to attend Eastern Mennonite College, where he earned a degree in biology in 1971. He attended medical school in the 1970s at the Hershey Medical Center, Pennsylvania State College, specializing in neurosurgery. After starting work as a physician, and looking to reduce stress after long workdays, Lee enrolled in a ceramics class at James Madison University in Harrisonburg, Virginia. It was there that he found the two passions of his life: studio pottery and his future bride, Holly, a jewelry designer. Lee enrolled in the school's ceramics master's program and received his degree in 1976.

From the start, Lee and his wife have sold their own work. Their first gallery was in Arlington, Virginia, followed by the Georgetown section of Washington, DC. They currently live near Stevens, Pennsylvania, and sell work directly from their studio or at major craft shows such as the ACC Baltimore Show, the Philadelphia Museum of Art Craft Show, and the Smithsonian Craft Show. In 1993, President and Mrs. Clinton invited Lee to contribute to the White House Collection of American Crafts, an exhibition that toured the country. Lee's work is now included in the permanent collections of several museums, including the Smithsonian American Art Museum's Renwick Gallery; the Mint Museum of Craft + Design, Charlotte, NC; Yale University Art Gallery, New Haven, CT; and the Racine Art Museum, Wisconsin. He has received numerous awards at craft shows. His work has been exhibited around the world and featured in publications, including *Craft in America: Celebrating Two Centuries of Artists and Objects* (2007) and the subsequent television series.

judith schaechter

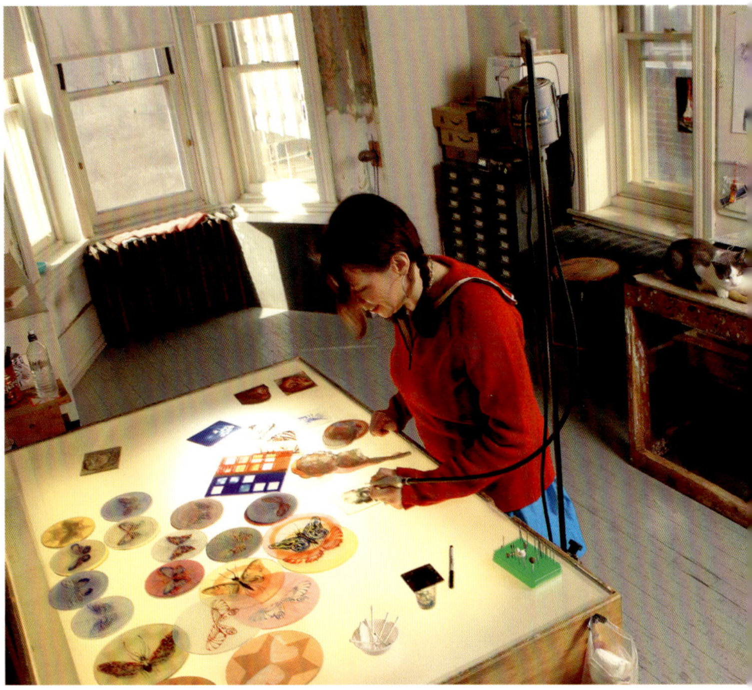

Judith Schaechter was born in 1961 in Gainesville, Florida, and grew up in Newton, Massachusetts. She remembers visiting the Museum of Fine Arts, Boston, as a child with her parents, where she particularly liked looking at Gothic art. Schaechter's work today reflects the influence of this imagery, as well as other sources such as cartoons, comic books, TV, design, history, and music, especially the expressive ideas found in the lyrics of new wave and punk rock.

Schaechter started her BFA training in 1979 as a painting major at the Rhode Island School of Design, in Providence. During her sophomore year, she took an elective stained glass class with Richard Harned and graduate student Ursula Huth, an experience that changed the direction of her artistic career. She switched her major to glass and graduated from RISD in 1983. The challenge of learning the technical skills to master a medium not many people had considered using for composing personal narratives excited and ignited her creative impulses. Today, Schaechter is known nationally and internationally for her stained glass pieces and as an innovator in the field.

Schaechter has received numerous awards and fellowships, among them a John Simon Guggenheim Fellowship, two grants from the National Endowment for the Arts, and a Louis Comfort Tiffany Foundation Award. Her work has been in many solo and group exhibitions, most recently at the Claire Oliver Gallery in New York and at the Contemporary Art Center of Virginia in Virginia Beach. Her work can be found in the permanent collections of American and European museums, including the Philadelphia Museum of Art in Pennsylvania, the Victoria & Albert Museum in London, and the Metropolitan Museum of Art and the Museum of Arts and Design in New York. She also had work featured in the Renwick's *Glassworks* exhibition in 1990 and in the 2002 Whitney Biennial. Schaechter maintains a studio in Philadelphia.

matthias pliessnig

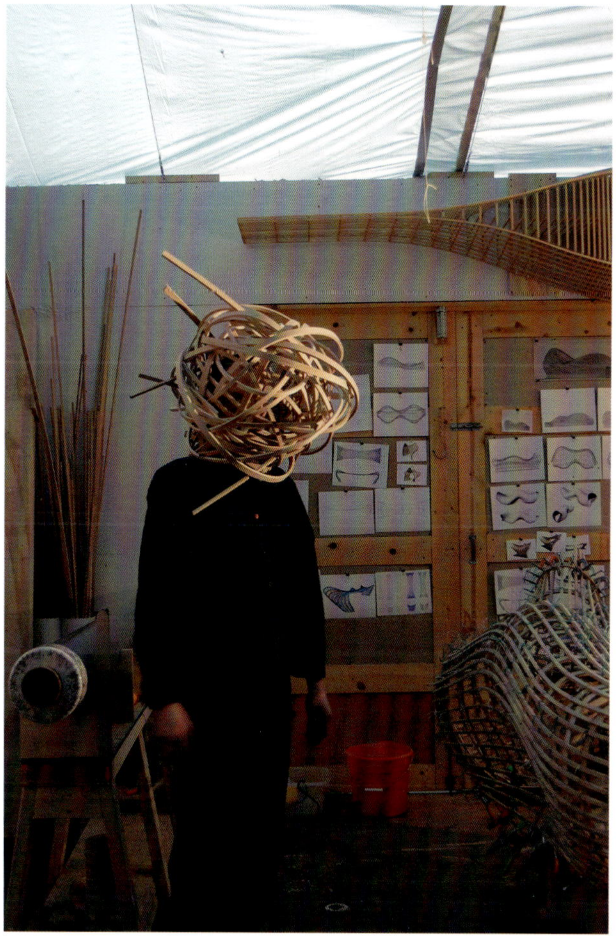

Born in New Orleans in 1978, Pliessnig as a child was interested in aviation, drawing, and knowing what made things work. He started his art education in the sculpture department at the Kansas City Art Institute and then transferred to the furniture department of the Rhode Island School of Design. It was there that he developed his penchant for woodworking and discovered the sympathetic relationship between design software and craft processes. After graduating from RISD in 2003, Pliessnig stayed in Providence, doing commission work for architects and occasionally exhibiting pieces in shows. He also became interested in boat design. While completing his MFA at the University of Wisconsin–Madison (2005–8), Pliessnig undertook a boat-building project with Professor Tom Loeser and fellow graduate student Benjamin Wooten that dramatically altered the direction of his work. The marine design–influenced pieces created since that experience have been exhibited and published widely over the last five years.

Pliessnig received grants in 2008 and 2009 from the Joan Mitchell Foundation and the Louis Comfort Tiffany Foundation, respectively. In 2008, *Interior Design Magazine* recognized *Providence* with a Best of Year award for lounge seating. His work is in the collection of the Museum of Arts and Design, New York. Pliessnig currently maintains his studio in Philadelphia.

exhibition checklist

Dimensions are given as height × width × depth.
Works marked with an asterisk (*) are not in the exhibition.

ubaldo vitali

Kiliaen van Rensselaer (1663–1719)
Teapot, about 1683–95
silver and wood
7 1/4 × 8 1/4 × 5 in.
Collection of the New-York Historical Society, Bequest of Major Philip Schuyler, 1915.20

Chamberstick with Upswept Handle, 1976
silver
3 7/16 × 6 1/2 × 4 1/8 in.
Collection of the artist

Crab and Urchin Candlestick, about 1976
silver
2 1/8 × 8 1/4 × 6 1/4 in.
Collection of the artist

Ribbed Conical Bowl, 1976
silver
2 3/4 × 5 1/4 in. diam.
Collection of the artist

Singerie Candlestick, about 1976
silver
6 1/4 × 4 3/8 × 5 1/8 in.
Collection of the artist

Cup, 1980
silver and gilding
4 × 4 3/4 in.
Collection of the Newark Museum, Gift of the artist, 1984, 84.10

Sketch for *Tureen*, 1980s
paper
8 1/2 × 11 in.
Collection of Dr. John Batzel

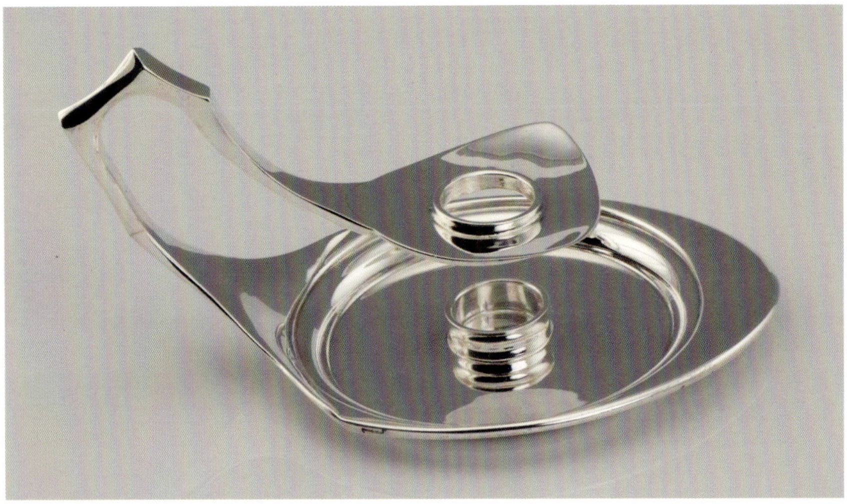

Coffee and Tea Service, 1983–84
silver, ebony, ivory, and Plexiglas
tray: 33 1/2 × 15 in.
coffeepot: 11 × 8 1/2 in.
teapot: 8 1/2 × 9 in.
creamer: 6 5/8 × 7 1/2 in.
sugar bowl: 6 5/8 × 10 in.
waste basin: 5 1/4 × 6 in.
Collection of the Newark Museum, Purchase 1984 The Members' Fund, 84.1

Centerpiece, 1986
sterling silver, silver gilt, bleached maple, and glass
18 1/4 × 14 × 14 1/4 in.
Collection of the Yale University Art Gallery, Janet and Simeon Braguin Fund, 2007.181.1

Pitcher, 1988
silver, bleached maple, and glass
10 1/4 × 4 3/4 × 9 3/4 in.
Collection of the artist

"Baroque Church" Pitcher, 1989
silver and glass
9 × 6 1/2 × 6 1/16 in.
Collection of the artist

Covered Tureen with Stand, 1989–90
sterling silver and ebony
6 1/4 × 21 1/2 × 13 in.
The Museum of Fine Arts, Houston, Museum purchase with funds provided by the National Endowment for the Arts, with gifts of the Interior Resource Center, William J. Hill and John G. Middleton, 90.372.a–c

Doodles and sketches, 1990s
paper
9 1/2 × 11 in.
Collection of the artist

50th Anniversary Centerpiece, 1994
silver and glass
24 × 20 in. diam.
Collection of Mrs. Iris Schwartz

Mondrian Bowl, 1999
patinated bronze and silver plate
5 1/8 × 11 3/4 × 11 3/4 in.
Collection of the artist

Ubaldo Vitali, *Chamberstick with Upswept Handle*, 1976, Collection of the artist

Cliff Lee, *Plate*, 1992, Collection of the artist

T-form Two-Light Candelabrum, 1999
silver and glass
12 1/4 × 9 3/4 × 4 1/4 in.
Collection of the artist

Triple Wave Pitcher, 1999
silver and ebony
8 7/16 × 11 1/8 × 4 7/16 in. diam.
Collection of the artist

*Sketch for *The Meadowlands Pace Trophy*, 2000
paper vellum
8 1/2 × 11 in.
Collection of the artist

**The Meadowlands Pace Trophy*, 2000
silver and wood
15 11/16 × 13 5/16 in. diam.
Collection of the artist

Tureen, 2001
silver and sodalite
6 1/4 × 21 1/4 × 13 in.
Collection of the artist

25th Anniversary Tea and Coffee Service, 2004 (designed in 1999)
silver and glass (glass by Leonard DiNardo)
(all pieces: in. diam.)
tray: 4 × 19 × 16 9/16
sugar bowl: 5 3/4 × 6 7/16
creamer (no lid): 4 × 5 7/8
coffeepot: 13 1/16 × 7 3/8
teapot: 9 13/16 × 8 3/16
Collection of Janet and Ricardo Zapata

cliff lee

Plate, 1992
porcelain, *guan* glaze, peach bloom glaze, and india ink
2 × 9 1/4 in. diam.
Collection of the artist

Guan-ware Vase, 1994
porcelain, *guan* glaze, and india ink
7 1/2 × 13 in. diam.
Smithsonian American Art Museum, Gift of Carol and Bill Wright in memory of Dr. Edward L. Katz, 2010.36.5

Lotus Bowl, 2000
porcelain and ivory celadon glaze
6 × 5 in. diam.
Collection of the artist

Lotus Bowl, 2000
porcelain and ivory celadon glaze
5 1/2 × 5 in. diam.
Collection of the artist

Teardrop, 2000
porcelain, *guan* glaze, and india ink
10 × 9 in. diam.
Collection of Irwin and Marilyn Scher

Teardrop, 2000
porcelain and *temmoku* glaze
8 3/4 × 7 3/4 in. diam.
Collection of the artist

Anniversary Tea Set, 2001
porcelain, imperial yellow glaze, and silver (silver handle by Holly Lee)
teapot: 7 3/4 × 9 1/4 × 6 7/8 in.
tea caddy: 7 3/4 × 4 in. diam.
sugar: 3 1/2 × 4 1/2 in diam.
5 cups: 2 3/4 × 3 1/2 in. diam.
Collection of Dr. Todd and Lisa Hoover

Teardrop, 2001
porcelain and imperial yellow glaze
14 1/4 × 5 1/2 in. diam.
Collection of the artist

Teardrop, 2001
porcelain and oxblood glaze
14 1/2 × 5 3/4 in. diam.
Collection of the artist

Teardrop, 2001
porcelain and *temmoku* glaze
6 × 6 1/2 in. diam.
Collection of the artist

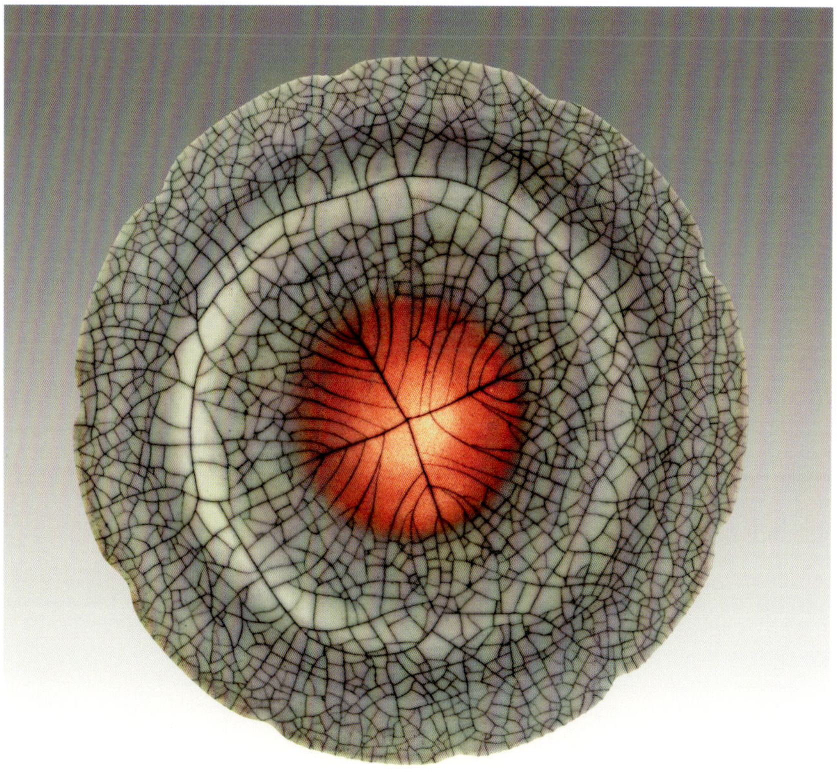

Table Set, 2002–8
porcelain and celadon glaze
(all pieces: in. diam.)
a: 5 1/2 × 4
b: 4 1/2 × 4
c: 4 1/2 × 3 1/2
d: 2 1/4 × 3
e: 2 1/4 × 2 1/4
f: 2 × 2
g: 2 × 1 1/2
h: 3 × 2 1/2
i: 4 3/4 × 1 1/2
Collection of the artist

Teardrop, 2004
porcelain and *chun* blue glaze
13 × 5 1/2 in. diam.
Collection of the artist

Teardrop, 2004
porcelain and tea dust glaze
12 × 12 in. diam.
Collection of the artist

Kiln Notebook, 2005–10
bound paper
11 × 8 1/2 in.
Collection of the artist

Peach, 2005
porcelain and celadon glaze
15 1/2 × 10 in. diam.
Collection of the artist

Teardrop, 2005
porcelain and peach bloom glaze
11 1/2 × 5 in. diam.
Collection of the artist

Prickly Melon, 2008
porcelain and imperial yellow glaze
11 × 7 in. diam.
Collection of the artist

Prickly Melon, 2008
porcelain and imperial yellow glaze
13 1/2 × 6 1/2 in. diam.
Collection of the artist

Lotus Vase with Flower, 2009
porcelain and celadon glaze
13 × 6 in. diam.
Collection of the artist

Double Dragon on Cloud Pedestal, 2009
porcelain, celadon glaze, and rubies
16 3/4 × 9 7/8 in. diam.
Collection of the artist

Luster Oilspot, 2010
porcelain and luster oilspot glaze
11 × 7 in. diam.
Collection of Carol A. Weiser and
George H. Weidner, Jr.

Lychee Nut Urn, 2010
porcelain and lava glaze
24 1/4 × 10 1/2 in. diam.
Collection of the artist

Lychee Nut Urn, 2010
porcelain and lava glaze
24 1/4 × 9 in. diam.
Collection of the artist

judith schaechter

Photographer unknown
John Fletcher Hamlin, 1863
paper, 3 3/4 × 2 1/4 in.
Collection of the artist

Sketch for *A Little Torcher*, 1990
paper
18 × 23 1/2 in.
Collection of Elmerina and Paul Parkman

A Little Torcher, 1990
glass
24 × 30 1/2 × 5 in.
Smithsonian American Art Museum,
Gift of the James Renwick Alliance
and museum purchase through the
Smithsonian Institution Collections
Acquisition Program, 1991.83

Judith and the Head of Holofernes, 2002
glass
45 × 17 × 6 in.
Collection of Ali K. Fard and Edward
Simpson

John Fletcher Hamlin Is No More, 2003
glass
35 × 36 × 6 in.
Collection of Dr. David Mittleman and
Mr. Hugh Glatts

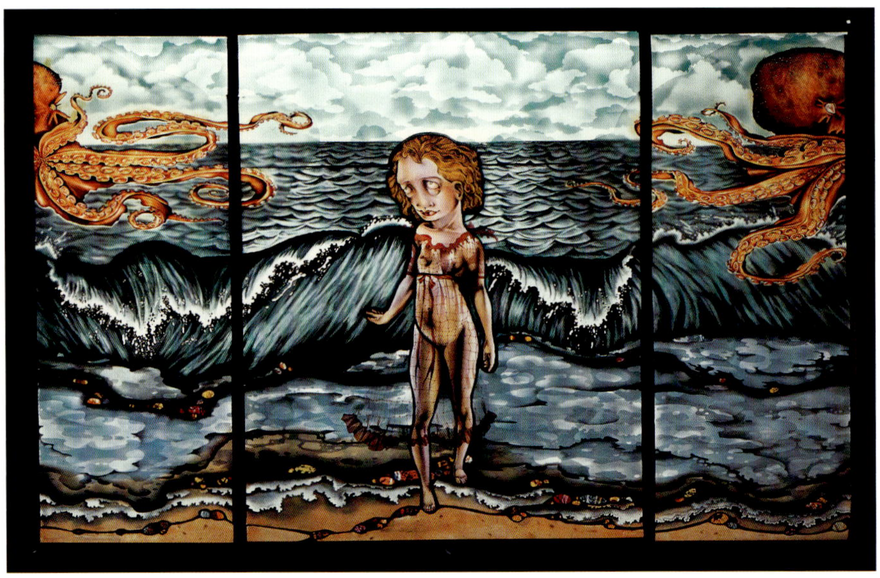

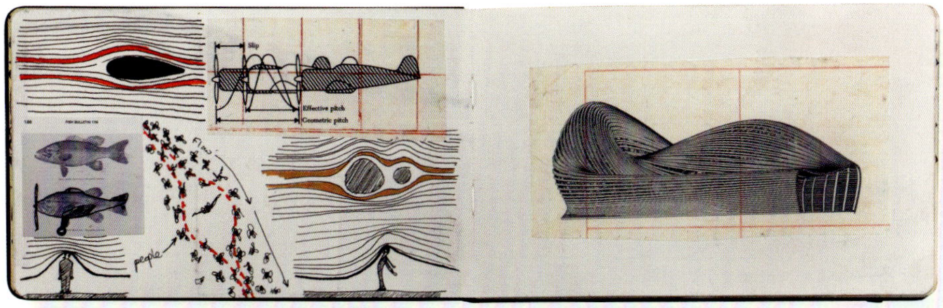

Dream of the Fisherman's Wife, 2004
stained glass in lightbox
32 × 48 × 6 in.
Collection of the Carnegie Museum of Art, Pittsburgh; Ailsa Mellon Bruce Fund, 2005.6

The Floor, 2006
glass
36 × 34 × 6 in.
Collection of Claire Oliver and Ian Rubinstein

Monument, 2006
glass
25 × 30 × 6 in.
Collection of Ryan and Joanna Scott

My One Desire, 2007
glass
35 × 52 × 6 in.
Collection of Todd Alios VonBastiaans

Sketch for *Widow*, 2008
graphite on paper
24 × 50 in.
Courtesy of Claire Oliver Gallery, New York

Widow, 2008
glass
24 × 28 × 6 in.
Collection of Colleen and John Kotelly

An Invocation, 2009
glass
26 × 34 × 6 in.
Courtesy of the artist and Claire Oliver Gallery, New York

Self-Portrait of Someone Else, 2009
glass
24 × 23 × 6 in.
Private collection

Holy Fool, 2009
graphite on paper
13 × 22 in.
Courtesy of the artist and Claire Oliver Gallery, New York

The Sin Eater, 2010
glass
25 × 46 × 6 in.
Courtesy of the artist and Claire Oliver Gallery, New York

matthias pliessnig

Artist's sketchbooks, 2006; 2010
bound paper
$8\frac{1}{4} \times 5\frac{1}{4}$; $8\frac{1}{4} \times 5$ in.
Collection of the artist

Bends, 2006
white oak
28 × 44 × 30 in.
Courtesy of Lewis Wexler, Wexler Gallery, Philadelphia

Thonet No. 18, 2007
white oak and Thonet No. 18 café chair
42 × 22 × 27 in.
Courtesy of Lewis Wexler, Wexler Gallery, Philadelphia

Waive, 2007
white oak
31 × 45 × 35 in.
Collection of Lorraine W. Hilleman

Rivulet, 2009
white oak and bamboo
28 × 96 × 35 in.
Private collection

Amada, 2010
white oak
35 in. × 16 ft. × 10 ft.
Private collection

Drift, 2010
white oak
$30\frac{1}{2} \times 114\frac{1}{2} \times 40$ in.
Collection of the artist

Judith Schaechter, *Dream of the Fisherman's Wife*, 2004, Carnegie Museum of Art, Pittsburgh

Matthias Pliessnig, artist's sketchbook, 2010

selected bibliography

Athineos, Doris. "Porcelain Perfection." *Traditional Home*, September 2000, 72–78.

Ayers, John, Margaret Medley, and Nigel Wood. *Iron in the Fire: The Chinese Potters' Exploration of Iron Oxide Glazes*. London: Oriental Ceramic Society, 1988.

Baker, Alex. Foreword in *Extra Virgin: The Stained Glass of Judith Schaechter*. Philadelphia: Free News Projects, 2006.

Barquist, David L. *Myer Myers: A Jewish Silversmith in Colonial New York*. With essays by Jon Butler and Jonathan D. Sarna. New Haven: Yale University Press, 2001.

Bell, Nicholas R. "An Ark of the New Republic." In *American Furniture 2009*. Edited by Luke Beckerdite. Milwaukee, WI: Chipstone Foundation, 2010.

———. *A Revolution in Wood: The Bresler Collection*. Washington, DC: Smithsonian American Art Museum, 2010.

Czernis-Ryl, Eva. *Contemporary Silver: Made in Italy*. Sydney, Australia: Powerhouse Publishing; Hampshire, UK: Lund Humphries, 2004.

Dauer, Paul F. "Cliff Lee: New Directions." *Ceramics Monthly* 47, no. 6 (June/July/August 1999): 52–56.

De Filippis, Marybeth, Peter N. Miller, and Deborah L. Krohn. *Dutch New York between East and West: The World of Margrieta van Varick*. New Haven: Yale University Press, 2009.

Dietrich, Lucas. *60. Innovators Shaping Our Creative Future*. London: Thames & Hudson, 2009.

Dietz, Ulysses Grant, ed. *The Glitter and the Gold: Fashioning America's Jewelry*. Newark, NJ: Newark Museum, 1997.

———. *Great Pots: Contemporary Ceramics from Function to Fantasy*. With an introduction by Garth Clark and Mark Del Vecchio. Madison, WI: Guild Publishing, 2003.

———. *Masterpieces of Art Pottery: 1880–1930*. Newark, NJ: Newark Museum, 2009.

———. *The Newark Museum Collection of American Art Pottery*. Newark, NJ: Newark Museum, 1984.

———. *Paul Stankard: Homage to Nature*. New York: Harry N. Abrams, 1996.

Dietz, Ulysses Grant, and Sam Watters. *Dream House: The White House as an American Home*. New York: Acanthus Press, 2009.

Dietz, Ulysses Grant et al. *Tiffany Retrospective: Designs from Tiffany & Co., 1837–1999*. Tokyo: APT International, 1999.

Dinwoodie, J. M. Wood: *Nature's Cellular, Polymeric Fibre-Composite*. London: Metal Institute, 1989.

D'Urfé, Honoré. *Astrea (L'Astrée)*, Vol. 1. Edited and translated by Steven Rendall. Binghamton, NY: Center for Medieval and Early Renaissance Studies, 1995.

Evans, Nancy Goyne. *Windsor-Chair Making in America: From Craft Shop to Consumer*. Hanover, NH: University Press of New England, 2006.

Falino, Jeannine, and Gerald Ward, eds. *Silver of the Americas, 1600–2000: American Silver in the Museum of Fine Arts, Boston*. Boston: MFA Publications, 2008.

Finegold, Rupert, and William Seitz. *Silversmithing*. Radnor, PA: Chilton Book Co., 1983.

Finlay, Robert. *The Pilgrim Art: Cultures of Porcelain in World History*. Berkeley: University of California Press, 2010.

Fitzgerald, Oscar P. *Studio Furniture of the Renwick Gallery, Smithsonian American Art Museum*. Washington, DC: Smithsonian American Art Museum, 2008.

Fuhring, Peter. "Juste-Aurèle Meissonnier and His Patrons." In *Rococo: The Continuing Curve, 1730–2008*, by Sarah D. Coffin et al. New York: Cooper-Hewitt, National Design Museum, Smithsonian Institution, 2008.

Fuller, Kate Baden. *Contemporary Stained Glass Artists: A Selection of Artists Worldwide.* London: A & C Black, 2006.

Gebrüder Thonet. *Thonet Bentwood & Other Furniture: The 1904 Illustrated Catalogue, with the 1905–6 and 1907 Supplements and Price Lists in German and English.* With a new introduction by Christopher Wilk. New York: Dover Publications, 1980.

Guo li gu gong bo wu yuan. *Masterworks of Chinese Porcelain in the National Palace Museum.* Taipei: National Palace Museum, 1970.

Herman, Lloyd E. *American Porcelain: New Expressions in an Ancient Art.* Forest Grove, OR: Timber Press, 1980.

Kelsey, John, ed. *Fine Woodworking on Bending Wood.* Newtown, CT: Taunton Press, 1985.

———. *Furniture Makers Explore Digital Technologies.* Furniture Studio Series. Free Union, VA: Furniture Society, 2005.

———. *The Meaning of Craft.* Furniture Studio Series. Free Union, VA: Furniture Society, 2006.

Lawrence, Lee. "In Search of the Perfect Form." *American Style Magazine,* no. 73 (Fall 2010): 54–59.

McCarthy, Cathleen. "Delicate Transformation." *Art & Antiques* 29, no. 12 (December 2006): 43–46.

Mino, Yutaka, and Katherine R. Tsiang. *Ice and Green Clouds: Traditions of Chinese Celadon.* Indianapolis: Indianapolis Museum of Art; Bloomington: Indiana University Press, 1986.

Monroe, Michael W. *The White House Collection of American Crafts.* New York: Harry N. Abrams, 1995.

Mowry, Robert D. *Hare's Fur, Tortoiseshell, and Partridge Feathers: Chinese Brown- and Black-Glazed Ceramics, 400–1400.* With contributions by Eugene Farrell and Nicole Coolidge Rousmaniere. Cambridge, MA: Harvard Art Museums, 1996.

Opie, Jennifer Hawkins. "Introducing Judith Schaechter." American issue, *Journal of Stained Glass* 28 (2005): 122–27, 201.

Ostergard, Derek E., ed. *Bent Wood and Metal Furniture, 1850–1946.* Seattle: University of Washington Press; New York: American Federation of Arts, 1987.

Page, Andrew. "Everything is Sacred." *Glass: The Urban Glass Quarterly,* no. 113 (Winter 2008/2009): 38–45.

Pierson, Stacey. *Earth, Fire and Water: Chinese Ceramic Technology. A Handbook for Non-Specialists.* London: University of London, Percival David Foundation of Chinese Art, 1996.

Podmaniczky, Michael. "The Incredible Elastic Chairs of Samuel Gragg." *The Magazine Antiques* 163, pt. 5 (2003): 138–51.

Raguin, Virginia Chieffo. *Stained Glass: From Its Origins to the Present.* New York: Harry N. Abrams, 2003.

Rössel, Greg. *Building Small Boats.* Brooklin, ME: WoodenBoat Publications, 2000.

Ruhlman, Michael. *Wooden Boats: In Pursuit of the Perfect Craft at an American Boatyard.* New York: Viking, 2001.

Schaechter, Judith. "Sustaining Stained Glass." *Glass: The Urban Glass Quarterly,* no. 92 (Fall 2003): 46–53.

Scott, Rosemary E., ed. *Chinese Copper Red Wares.* Percival David Foundation of Chinese Art Monograph Series 3. London: The Foundation, 1992.

Shallcross, Gilian. *Masterpieces: Great Paintings of the World in the Museum of Fine Arts, Boston.* Boston: MFA Publications, 2008.

Stern, Jewel. *Modernism in American Silver: 20th-Century Design.* Edited by Kevin W. Tucker and Charles Venable. New Haven: Yale University Press, 2005.

Sullivan, Robert. "Through the Looking Glass." *American Craft* 69, no. 1 (February/March 2009): 62–69.

Vainker, S. J. *Chinese Pottery and Porcelain: From Prehistory to the Present.* New York: George Braziller, 1991.

Vitali, Ubaldo. "Beyond the Secret Traditions: the Evolution of Style and Techniques in the Art of the Goldsmith." In *Silver Society Journal*, no. 12, 2000.

———, and Pete Dandridge. *Lions, Dragons, and Other Beasts: Aquamanilia of the Middle Ages, Vessels for Church and Table.* DVD. Edited by Peter Burnet and Pete Dandridge. New York: Metropolitan Museum of Art; New Haven: Yale University Press, 2006.

———. "Meissonnier's Goldsmith Persona: A Sublimation of Forms and Techniques, *Natura ed Invenzione*." In *The Thyssen Meissonnier Silver Tureen.* New York: Sotheby's, 1998.

———. "A Quest for the Domus Aurea in the Resurgence of Gilding." In *Antiquity Revisited: English and French Silver-Gilt from the Collection of Audrey Love*, by Anthony Phillips and Jeanne Sloane. London: Christie's, 1997.

———. "Retooling for the Rococo: Assembling the Complex Network of Talents, Skill and Language to Express the New Style." In *Rococo Silver in England and Its Colonies: Papers from a Symposium at Virginia Museum of Fine Arts, Richmond, 2004.* London: Silver Society, 2006.

Von Vegesack, Alexander, et al. *Thonet: Classic Furniture in Bent Wood and Tubular Steel.* New York: Rizzoli, 1997.

Waggoner, Shawn. "Transforming Pain into Beauty." *Glass Art* 19, no. 6 (September/October 2004): 6–19.

Wagner, Andrew. "Craft: It's What You Make of It." In *Handmade Nation: The Rise of DIY, Art, Craft, and Design*, by Faythe Levine and Cortney Heimerl. New York: Princeton Architectural Press, 2008.

Wood, Nigel. *Chinese Glazes: Their Origins, Chemistry, and Recreation.* London: A & C Black; Philadelphia: University of Pennsylvania Press, 1999.

Zhu, Yan, jin shi. *Description of Chinese Pottery and Porcelain: Being a Translation of the T'ao Shuo.* With introduction, notes, and a bibliography by Stephen W. Bushell. Oxford: Clarendon Press, 1910.

image credits

All photography by Gene Young except as noted. All Judith Schaechter images: courtesy of the artist, photography by Dominic Episcopo.

Figs. 5, 7, 11: courtesy of Ubaldo Vitali, Inc.; fig. 6: courtesy the New-York Historical Society; fig. 12: The Museum of Fine Arts, Houston; photo by Thomas R. DuBrock; fig. 13: © Yale University Art Gallery; fig. 17: courtesy Philadelphia Museum of Art; fig. 23: Freer Gallery of Art, photo by Robert Harrell; fig. 32: Freer Gallery of Art, photo by Neil Greentree; fig. 36: photograph © 2010 Museum of Fine Arts, Boston; fig. 48: photo by Matthias Pliessnig; figs. 49, 53–55: drawings by Matthias Pliessnig, courtesy of the artist; fig. 58: courtesy, The Winterthur Library, Printed Book and Periodical Collection; p. 94: 1961 photo by Aldo Vitali; p. 95: photo by Douglas Lee; p. 96: courtesy of the artist; p. 97: photo by Matthias Pliessnig; p. 100: image © 2004 Judith Schaechter

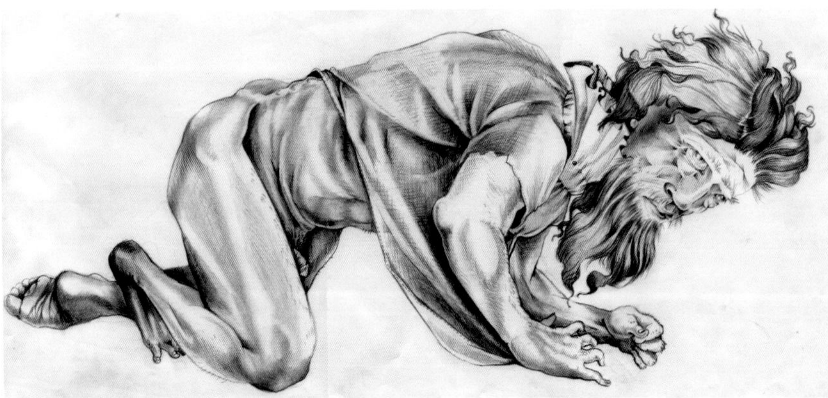

Judith Schaechter, *Holy Fool*, 2009, Courtesy of the artist and Claire Oliver Gallery, New York